To H. M. Stone,
with thanks and
best wishes,

Irene. J. Johnson.

TURNING POINT:

The Story of
Kirby Le Soken, Essex
1823 to 1862

The Reverend William Burgess, B.D., Vicar and Commissary of the Sokens of Thorpe, Kirby and Walton 1823-1862.

By Courtesy of the Vicar of Thorpe.

TURNING POINT:
The Story of
Kirby le Soken, Essex
1823 to 1862

by

Irene Johnson

Regency Press (London & New York) Ltd.
125 High Holborn, London WC1V 6QA

ISBN 0 7212 0651 4

Printed and bound in Great Britain by
Buckland Press Ltd., Dover, Kent.

Author's Note

This is not a scholarly work, but the story of the people of Kirby le Soken in their finest hour and told with the help of their descendants. I wish to thank Nancy Briggs, M.A., Supervisor of the Students' Room of the Essex Record Office and her staff for their continuous help, my sister Winifred M. Johnson who made it possible to search the many areas involved and advised on music. My thanks to Paula Brown and Ian Freeborn for their assistance and my friends in Kirby Cross for their encouragement. Facilities for research have been most generous. I am grateful to A. C. Edwards who has read the script and advised on publication.

Sources

I *Primary Sources consulted at:—*
1. *County Record Offices:*
   Cambridge, Essex, Exeter, London, Northampton, Norwich.
2. Cambridge University Library; Guildhall Library of the City of London.
3. *National Archives:*
   British Museum Library; India Library and Archives; Public Record Office.
4. *Civic Library Collections:*
   Birmingham; Chelmsford; Colchester; Hackney; Leamington.
5. *Private Collections:*
   British and Foreign Bible Society; Church Missionary Society; Royal Institute of British Architects; Royal School of Church Music; St. Bartholomew's Hospital.
6. *Information from Records supplied by:*
   Bank of England; National Provincial Bank; The Royal Society.
   Schools: St. John's, Leatherhead; St. Mary's Hall, Brighton.
   Metropolitan Museum of New York.
7. *Parish Registers at the Church:*
   Sokens of Thorpe, Kirby and Walton.
   Maidwell; Willingham; Oakhampton.
8. *Kirby le Soken*
   The Vicar of St. Michael's, the Reverend Peter Garner.

Virginia ~~Joan~~ Franklin.

II *Information from Descendants*
   B. W. Stone; H. Marjorie Stone; Marguerite Everard; Frederick A. Baker; K. J. Abercrombie; Francis A. Almond; Robert and Paula Baker; Joan Bamford; Kate Dore.

III *Secondary Sources*
   The End of the Soken Court. E. A. Wood.
   The Baker Family in India. Eira Dalton (C.M.S. Kottayam 1963).

The Choral Revival in the Anglican Church 1839 to 1872 by Bernarr Rainbow (Barry and Jenkins 1970).
The Dictionary of National Biography.
Social Discontent and Agrarian Disturbances in Essex 1795-1850. S. W. Amos 1971 (M.A. Thesis E.R.O.).

Contents

List of Illustrations

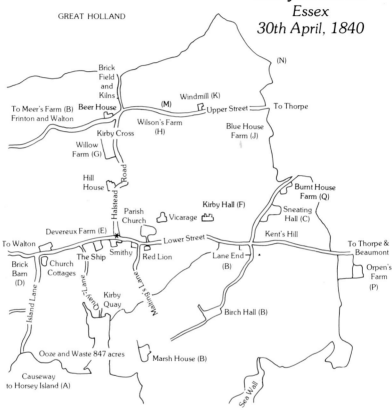

Parish of
Kirby Le Soken
Essex
30th April, 1840

GREAT HOLLAND

Brick Field and Kilns

Windmill (K)

(N)

To Meer's Farm (B) Frinton and Walton

Beer House

(M)

Upper Street

To Thorpe

Wilson's Farm (H)

Kirby Cross

Blue House Farm (J)

Willow Farm (G)

Halstead Road

Hill House

Burnt House Farm (Q)

Parish Church

Vicarage

Kirby Hall (F)

Sneating Hall (C)

Devereux Farm (E)

Kent's Hill

To Walton

Lower Street

To Thorpe & Beaumont

The Ship

Smithy

Red Lion

Lane End (B)

Orpen's Farm (P)

Brick Barn (D)

Church Cottages

Island Lane

Quay Lane

Kirby Quay

Maling's Lane

Birch Hall (B)

Ooze and Waste 847 acres

Marsh House (B)

Causeway to Horsey Island (A)

Sea Wall

KEY:— FARMERS

(A) Henry Blanchard (Owner).
(B) Samuel Baker.
(C) Jeremiah Foaker.
(D) John Dennis Daniels.
(E) William Warner (Coal Merchant).
(F) Robert Mumford.
(G) Richard Stone.
(H) William Wilson (doubt about Farm's name).

(J) James Coates.
(K) John Wilson (Miller).
(L) Joseph Hughes (Maltster).
(M) George Snare.
(N) William Tillett.
(P) Daniel Orpen.
(Q) William King.
★ The Cage

Other Leading Inhabitants
John Daniels (Post Office).
Elizabeth Barnard (Landowner).
Ambrose Low (Butcher).
Thomas Bundock (Butcher, Constable).
John Gifford (Small builder).

CHAPTER ONE

The Village 1823

'You are appointed by the laws, not to act as the conscientious guardians of the property and interests of the church, but for the express purpose of aiding and assisting in the management of its temporal affairs.'

(William Burgess to Churchwardens, 1825)

The name 'Kirby' is of Danish origin, meaning 'by the church' and the three Sokens of Kirby, Thorpe and Walton formed a Peculiar Jurisdiction or Soke granted some time before 941 by the Saxon kings to the Dean and Chapter of St. Paul's in London, under the name of Eudulphesna or Alduleuesnasa; today the seal is in the British Museum and the Stall in St. Paul's Cathedral remains. Like the monasteries and chantries, the dean and chapter lost power and property in the sixteenth century when papal authority was replaced by the king as head of the Church of England, and in 1551 the Sokens were granted by Edward VI to Sir Thomas Darcy who already owned the lands of the Priory of Saint Osyth. After several changes of ownership in the eighteenth century, the manorial rights were bought as a profitable investment on the 16th of February 1826, for £2,300 from the Reverend Thomas Scott by the Harwich solicitor, Mr. Benjamin Chapman, who became Lord of the Sokens with the Reverend William Burgess already the Commissary.

When the Reverend William Burgess was inducted in 1823, Kirby le Soken, including Peewit and Horsey Islands, had a population of over nine hundred in an area of 3,874 acres other than Saltings, and, except for Horsey Island where sheep grazed, was famous for its rich arable land producing mainly wheat and barley. An 1824 bill of sale describes the area as 'abounding with Hares and Partridges; only One Mile and a Half from Walton, a fashionable

Watering-Place; two miles from Thorpe; Thirteen miles from Colchester and Sixty four miles from the Metropolis'. Providing an easy link with the coasts of Essex, Suffolk and the Port of London 'the Quay or Wharf connecting Mercantile business with a Farming concern . . . is capable of containing Two Vessels . . . On a convenient part of the Wharf is a Corn Granary, a Dwelling House, Counting House, Lime Kiln and Lime House: Store House, Stable and enclosed Coal Yard'. Through this port, coal and chalk (for lime) were imported and grain exported and in most of the period 1823 to 1862 the tenant of Devereux Farm, William George Clark Warner, was both farmer and coal merchant; the harbour remained open until the defences of the 1939-45 War resulted in a large-scale silting-up. Today, other than the farm, only the dwelling house and the granary (now made into an attractive residence) remain.

The parish of Kirby le Soken (today on the B1054) was made up of the main Lower Street linked to Horsey Island by a causeway visible only at low tide, Upper Street, the hamlet of Kirby Cross and some uninhabited islands among the Saltings. To the north west from Kirby Quay across Hamford Water was the Thorpe Quay of Landermere and Walton Quay to the east, an ideal area for smuggling. As the name implies, the centre of village life was the church with the nearby red brick manor house of Kirby Hall. The population was employed in farming, with the complement of craftsmen necessary to village life: blacksmith, maltster, wheelwright, carpenter, collar-maker, miller, shoemaker, thatcher and bricklayer (the term given to a small builder), together with shops and inns. In Lower Kirby, at what is now White Rose Cottage, John Daniels kept the Post Office and controlled the carrier trade to Colchester and, with other shopkeepers, sold almost everything (other than butcher's meat) from candles to coffins; the Ship Inn was at the corner of Quay Lane and 'The Lion' (today 'The Red Lion') faced the Parish church. The Upper Street had its own shops, miller, blacksmith, the inn of 'The Hare and Hounds' and later a small Primitive Methodist Chapel, and by the 1830's Robert Button had opened a Beer Shop at Kirby Cross. With a good piece of land to grow vegetables and keep poultry, many cottages were small, with often one room upstairs and one down, usually of wattle and daub with plastered walls and a thatched roof; but the demand for brick grew in the early 1840's

12

with the development of the brickfields on the Holland Road almost opposite Dead Lane by the Suffolk-born John Cooper, the friend and business associate of the builder John Gifford of Kirby Cross. Shortage of water was virtually unknown because of the numerous underground springs especially in the area of Hill House and Willow Farm, and wells were sunk in all parts of the Parish; each dwelling disposed of its own sewage to manure the land. Church accounts make it clear that all its needs were met by village craftsmen and shopkeepers except for Communion wine, until the major rebuilding of 1832-33.

'The Peculiar Jurisdiction of Kirby, Thorpe and Walton le Soken in the Archdeaconry of Colchester, the Deanery and Hundred of Tendring' was exempt to the Commissary of the lord of the manor

The Centre of Kirby le Soken (about 1900) opposite the Church, showing The Red Lion and the adjoining shops as they were in 1841. From right to left: Ambrose Low (butcher); The Red Lion; Henry Lott's Grocer's shop and on the far left Thomas Bundock (butcher). The Red Lion was connected by an underground passage to the Saltings for religious refugees in the sixteenth century and used by smugglers. In 1946, the Brewers bricked in the passage which had become dangerous. Ambrose Low's cottage was demolished to make a Car Park.

Courtesy of J. Wilson.

Kirby le Soken—The Smithy of Lower Street from an early twentieth century postcard.

in all matters ecclesiastical except that of institution and induction which belonged to the Bishop (of London), and to whose visitation it was subject. Thus, until 1858, when Parliament deprived the Church of England of its control in such matters, for those living within the Sokens, the Vicar and Commissary granted marriage licences, proved wills and issued letters of administration as well as trying and punishing ecclesiastical offenders. This church court was held regularly at Michaelmas (September 29th), and every three weeks when necessary, in the chancel of Thorpe church with the steward of the manor of the Sokens sometimes acting as registrar.

In Kirby Hall, the lord of the manor or his steward held Court Baron on Saint Anne's day (July 26th) or whenever a special circumstance arose. The customs of the Soken listed in 1509 (see Appendix I) included the rule that 'The Court Rolls ought to be kept in a chest in Kirby Church, with three locks, one key to remain with the Lord, another with the Steward, and the third with the Tenants'; hence the three iron bands and padlocks on the parish chest today. The court dealt with the transfer of land and 'no learned man in the Law shall have any voice in the Court but only the Steward and Tenant'. By the nineteenth century, Kirby also included the small manors of Birch Hall and Sneating which held separate courts.

The nearest court of petty sessions was at Thorpe, but the parish constable used more direct methods to keep the peace in a village with regular shipping traffic. On a small green plot, in the middle of Halstead Road at the junction with the Lower Street, stood an iron cage, the foundations of which remained until after the 1914-18 war when the village war memorial was put on the site; later road-widening meant the removal of the war memorial and the end of the green. For years the parish constable used The Cage, not only to house prisoners awaiting trial at Thorpe or Chelmsford, but to lock up the drunk and unruly, a swift form of primitive justice which was effective and cheap. The use of the Cage was abandoned after the 1860's when the completion of the Tendring railway effectively linked the area to the petty sessions at Thorpe. To the left of what is now the church hall (as we face the building) stood a gallows tree, unused in the nineteenth century because serious cases went to the assize court at Chelmsford and the 1824 act of parliament abolished hanging for most crimes except murder and treason, so men were no longer hanged for sheep stealing.

Today, it is difficult to envisage the extent of the authority of the large scale tenant farmer in 1823, even though he had to wait until the passage of the 1832 Reform Bill to receive the right to elect a member of parliament. However, the Kirby parish vestry meeting of ratepayers not only chose one of the two churchwardens, but elected the overseer of the poor, the surveyor of highways who was responsible for the upkeep of roads, two assessors who decided the rateable value of property, and the constable, responsible for law and order. In addition, the leading inhabitants supplied a quota for the twenty four man jury of the Commission of Sewers for the Level of Tendring to investigate 'all Defects Defaults and Wants and Raparations of and in the Walls Banks Ditches Fences Sewers Gates Bridges Streams Watercourses Sluices Locks and other complements and annoyances'. A Kirby farmer was paid to act as an assistant overseer of the poor even when the 1834 Poor Law Amendment Act grouped the parishes into one Union with a single workhouse at Tendring, and a Tendring Hundred farmer, sometimes from Kirby, received a salary for acting as collector and expenditor to the commission of sewers for the Tendring Hundred. Annually, Kirby householders, other than cottagers, paid great tithe (total value £841. 0. 3. in 1840) to the Honeywood family the impropriator, tithes to the vicar (see chapter two), land tax at four shillings (20p) in the pound, poor rate, a rate for the upkeep of parish highways and another for sewers to protect the coastline; the last four were collected under the authority of two local justices of the peace sitting at Thorpe. The church rate, in contrast, was collected only when specially authorised by the parish vestry under the direction of the vicar and his churchwarden, and in 1831 this gave Samuel Baker of Birch Hall and Meers Farm, the opportunity to challenge the authority of the Reverend William Burgess as Commissary.

The 1598 Act of Settlement gave churchwardens and overseers the authority to examine and question anyone without real property who came to live in the village and therefore liable to be a charge on the parish, and a sworn statement was made before the two justices of the peace. Just as Kirby le Soken received back its original inhabitants, so orders of removal of intruders unable to prove their claim to be legal inhabitants was carried out. Most were farm labourers caught up in the change of employer with the

Kirby le Soken—The Church and the Reverend William Burgess's Vicarage from the grounds of Kirby Hall.

Photo: 'Two Js Photographic'

inevitable crossing of parish boundaries especially between Kirby, Thorpe, Frinton, Great Holland and Great Clacton, but even the builder John Gifford, born in Thorpe, married with a small family, had to seek legal acceptance on the 19th February 1812 before the justices of the peace.

Kirby overseers were willing to protect their own poor, but with a businesslike approach. It was cheaper to provide the sum for a special licence costing £2. 15s. (£2.75) for marriage than to maintain the illegitimate child and its mother! So in 1831, the sixteen year old John Baker of Great Holland, whose father, Henry, was under sentence of transportation for his part in the Tendring riots, married seventeen year old Elizabeth Powell of Kirby with the consent of their mothers as guardians, and the overseer Richard Stone of Willow Farm and the very efficient parish constable, Thomas Bundock, the butcher, witnessed the ceremony. Once John and Elizabeth were married, the family became the responsibility of Great Holland and Kirby ratepayers reaped the benefit. To increase efficiency, the vestry meeting of May 1815 had contracted to purchase for £200 a small farmhouse on the Lower Kirby Road (today the site of the modern 'Ash Trees') 'for a workhouse for the habitation and employment' of those poor unable to live on parish relief in a private household.

Every man between eighteen and forty-five years old and with an income sufficient to include most artisans, shopkeepers, farmers and private inhabitants, was on the militia list and liable for military service, unless physically handicapped, a licensed teacher or medical practitioner. Exemption was obtained by acting as special constable in an emergency and the practice of sending a stand-in was common. But, except for creating a favourable grain market and so increasing their prosperity, Kirby farmers were little affected by the long war with France which finally ended in 1815: Samuel Baker stopped a pound of a labourer's annual wage of fourteen because he went for two weeks training in the local militia in 1814 during the second year of his seven year contract.

Labourers were hired by farmers from the pool opposite the church or for a contracted wage and a period varying from one to seven years beginning at Michaelmas, with extra wages at harvest time. The wage for an able bodied labourer in 1823 was about fourteen pounds a year when living with his family on the premises

Kirby le Soken—Kirby Hall, the Manor House.
Photo: 'Two Js Photographic'

of his employer: Samuel Baker, for example, used Marsh Farm to house several of his labourers and their families. A contract with a farmer ensured a livelihood during the winter when threshing was done. One of the advantages of a farmer being elected surveyor of highways was that it provided well-paid work on the roads for his labourers during the winter and early spring, as well as a fee to farmers for the use of horses, waggons and two men to load and cart the almost inexhaustible supply of shingle brought by barge from Frinton beach. With the fall of grain prices, both farmers and men suffered: the one pound per day paid to farmers for a team in 1841 dropped to eight shillings (40p) after that date.

One of the most most intriguing aspects of Kirby life was the vital part played by the women. By English law, the property of a woman became that of her husband, but the manor of the Sokens was unusual in its practice of obtaining the separate consent of the wife to any transfer of land by her husband. So it was recognised that women had an active part to play, indeed some wives carried on the business after the death of their husbands: Samuel Baker's widow, Mary, continued farming Birch Hall; both Rebecca Harman Stone and then her daughter of the same name took over the late Richard Stone's 'Willow Farm'; Elizabeth Riddlesdell continued the blacksmith's business in Lower Kirby, employing two men after her husband's death. Like their husbands and brothers, they were educated at least in the three Rs, knowledgeable in farming practice and, in many cases, expert horsewomen. Judging by the furniture inherited from Frinton Hall and Willow Farm by the Stone family, their homes were well furnished and usually maintained with the help of two indoor female servants.

Good farm land, advantageous tenant rights and cheap transport brought an influx of tenant farmers and labourers (often unmarried) from Suffolk, so that little inbreeding resulted. At the beginning of our period, marriages in the farming community were arranged, and the bride's father provided a suitable dowry. So in 1808, the timber merchant, Robert Large of Great Clacton paid six hundred pounds for the marriage of his daughter, Mary, to Samuel Baker of Meers Farm, the eldest son of William, probably the wealthiest working farmer in the Kirby and Walton area.

When the Reverend William Burgess was instituted as vicar of the Sokens in 1823, the parish life of Kirby was dominated by a group of tenant farmers of whom the forty year old Samuel Baker (by 1830 tenant of Meers Farm, Marsh House, Lane End, Skippers and Birch Hall) was the most powerful. His father William, had come from East Bergholt in Suffolk and had worked as a tenant farmer in Great Holland. Wisely, William increased his wealth by a succession of marriages to Elizabeth Draper, daughter of the wealthy owner of Meers Farm and niece of Henry Draper of Hill House; to Mary Brown of Walton; finally to the twice-widowed Sarah Skipper. Short, dark, with deep-set eyes, William must have possessed great social charm as well as a capacity for hard work; for not only had he become the friend of Richard Stone of Frinton Hall and William Dennis of Brick Barn, but extended his influence by marrying his daughter, Elizabeth, to John Smith, and Frances to James Page (both of Great Clacton) and Mary to Thomas Stone from Landermere Hall, Thorpe, who later farmed first at Dunton and then at Horndon on the Hill. The younger children each inherited £1,400 on coming of age and, when necessary, were apprenticed to a trade. So in 1823 Samuel Baker was probably the most influential farmer in the area without any awkward family encumbrances.

The members of the Stone family came from Framfield in Sussex where they had been granted a coat of arms in 1628. By the second half of the eighteenth century, Richard Stone rented Frinton Hall where the family was to remain for over a century and in 1784 added the tenancy of Willow Farm adjoining the estate of Hill House, the land of which his son was later to rent. The men of the family were handsome, but, in contrast to the Bakers, tall and big-boned. When William Baker's friend, Richard Stone, died in 1821, his wealth had been depleted by paying off the debts of Thomas Stone of Landermere Hall, and his eldest son, Richard, about the same age as Samuel Baker, lacked Samuel's almost ruthless ambition. The Stone family was linked by marriage to the third

Kirby Quay 1970. The attractive dwelling house is made by developing The Granary, the last of the surviving buildings.

powerful farming family of William Dennis of Brick Barn (this family had come from the nearby Beaumont-cum-Moze), but in 1823 William Dennis was an old man. Childless, by the will drawn up in 1825, he made generous provision for his stepson, John Daniels, the postmaster, and adopted as his heir John Daniels' elder son, who by the time of William's death in 1829, was known as John Dennis Daniels.

So in 1823 Samuel Baker had all the opportunities and makings of a village dictator. The vicar's churchwarden, Benjamin Barton of Horsey Island, was nearly eighty, and the second warden, elderly. Hill House on the Halstead Road had become unimportant in village life after the death of Samuel's uncle Henry in 1807 with a succession of resident owners who were outsiders:—the Sparlings from Colchester until 1841 and later by the Shums from London; neither family held office under William Burgess. The independent attitude of the Kirby farmers was increased by the structure of the vestry meeting. Because the vicar of the Sokens lived in Thorpe, he seldom took the chair at Kirby and the curate was denied the privilege. So by 1823 the vicar's warden was regularly chairing the meeting, but the old Benjamin Barton was no match for Samuel Baker. Already Samuel had been churchwarden three times and his sense of importance was emphasised by his occupation of the special pew built for Gabriel Shaw in 1726 for family "assigns and successors occupying the farm or Mansion House called "Meerlands" (Meers Farm) in the eastern part of the church near the chancel.

Faced with this situation and the lack of response by the Kirby vestry meeting to his annual charge to the churchwardens to plan the repair of the church and re-organise the seating, William Burgess apparently rebuilt the churches of Thorpe and Walton and waited until the balance of power in Kirby le Soken changed, to ensure victory in his inevitable confrontation with Samuel Baker.

CUSTOMS AND HISTORY OF THE SOKEN

'These be the Customs that the Tenants of the Dean and Chapter of Pauls in London, videlt. of Thorpe Kerby and Walton, within the Socken, doe claim to hold, and have held beyond the Memory of Man'. 19th century copy of a certified copy, made 3 Sept. 1763 by Wm. Enefer of a custumal of 1509 'that came from Pauls in London'.

Claims are:—

1. Three weeks' notice of Courts and Leets.
2. To sell or give lands etc. without the lord's licence for a term of fifty years, and during that term to bequeath for a further fifty years.
3. That the heir of a tenant who has died, after alienating this term of fifty years, shall, after warning the buyer and paying the arrearages with his own goods, have the remainder of the term, and must fine with the lord.
4. That an heir not of age should be nourished by his mother (or next of kin chosen, to whom the land cannot come) and is to be referred to a purchaser if any part of the land is willed to be sold.
5. That any tenant in fee or in term may bequeathe the fee or term on his deathbed in the presence of one tenant of the manor.
6. That a tenant on his deathbed may sell land to satisfy debts, 'over and above his cattle'.
7. That every tenant ought to be judged by the tenants within the Socken, 'and that no learned man in the Law shall have any voice in the Court, but only the Steward and the tenants'.
8. That a widow ought within forty days to chose whether to pay a heriot and keep her Free Bench or to allow the heir to take the land: and if a second wife becomes a widow the Steward shall charge the Court to allow her as much of her husband's land as shall be thought meet. Similarly for husband of dead female tenants except the man shall pay no heriot.
9. 'Every tenant ought to be assigned to suit of Court one in plea of Transgression, 2d, in plea of Lands 3. and in plea of Land

the tenant ought to be distrained upon the lands by the space of fifteen days next before the Court in the presence of two witnesses being tenants of the same Town in which the Land lieth'.

10. That tenants may fish, hawk and take fowls on their own land without the lord's licence.

11. That damage to corn, meadow or pasture, shall be viewed by the Lord's Baylie with four or six tenants, and afterwards 'judged upon three others by the steward'.

12. That 'every tenant that is bound to thresh the lord's corn ought to see it measured and safely used'.

13. 'That the Court Rolls ought to be kept in a Chest in Kirby Church, with three locks, one key to remain with the Lord, another with the steward, and the third with the tenants'.

14. That only the Steward, clerk and the sworn offerers ought to be present at the Court.

15. That no stranger shall buy any Land within the Socken.

Kirby le Soken—
The Parish Chest.
Note the three locks.

16. That the lord's bailiff shall not distrain of any man's holding if he have goods or chattels to distrain otherwhere, unless for the lord's rent or service.
17. That no bailiff of the King shall enter the Liberty of the Socken to arrest any man without the presence and consent of the lord's Bailiff and the constable of the town.
18. That tenants' cattle may graze in the highways without the lord's licence: and tenants may 'cut down, root up and dispose at their pleasure' trees which they have planted on their own land.
19. 'That in the Harvest they shall be warned by the Bailiff before the sun go down, to come and keep the lord's corn the next morning.'
20. 'That in the Law day they shall be charged with but only articles concerning that Leet', except verdicts remaining undecided.
21. If the inquest of one town disagree about a title of land, thirty-six (i.e. a whole inquest from each town) may be chosen, and if they cannot agree, they ought to chose one two or three to determine the case.

CHAPTER TWO

The Reverend William Burgess

*'However success may seem to attend on those
who attempt to obstruct the cause of God and
hinder the efforts of his minister, the end of all
such attempts must be shame and confusion.'*

(William Burgess 1827)

The Reverend William Burgess was born probably at Manor Farm,
Maidwell near Northampton and christened at the parish church of
Saint Mary on the 15th January, 1780. His father, William, was
one of the five children of Jeremiah and Frances, but left his family
in Willingham, Cambridge, and went to nearby Hazlebeach,
Northamptonshire, where, like his father and twin brother John,
he was a gardener. There on the 4th April, 1779, William Burgess
married Diana, daughter of a small farmer, John Church of Manor
Farm and his wife Mary, by special licence.

Saint Mary and All Saints, Willingham, was a centre of religious
activity, unusual in a village church. Because of its position half
way between the university town of Cambridge within the diocese
of Ely and Ely cathedral, it was used regularly for the ordination of
clergy. There, judging from the terms of his will in 1862, in which
he left small legacies to all cousins surviving him, William Burgess
probably spent much of his youth with his uncle John who later left
him a hundred pounds, and his aunts Sarah (wife of John Barton)
and Mary (died in Cambridge 1802), and with his grandmother,
widowed three years before William was born. She died in July
1803 aged eighty five, by which date he was married and already
established as a prosperous grocer in Colchester, the capital of
north east Essex.

On the 17th of November 1797, when William Burgess was
nearly eighteen, the Reverend John Wykes, rector of Maidwell,
supplied him with a certificate of his baptism, but why it was

St. Michael's Church and Vicarage, Kirby le Soken. A Pastel Drawing by William Coxhead, grandson of The Reverend William Coxhead. Made at Hill House about 1905. (The picture is inaccurate—compare photograph on page 16.)
Courtesy of H. M. Stone.

needed at this date is a mystery. However, it is interesting that in the July of that year, Elizabeth King, second wife of Shaw King of Meers Farm, Kirby le Soken, became a widow and, other than William, remains the sole link between the Northampton area and Essex. When she married the wealthy and influential Shaw King, who owned large areas of East Essex, she brought as part of her dowry, lands in the parishes of Islip, Doddington Magna and Burton Latimer in the Northampton area, and could well have been the patroness of this young man. Probably, Burgess was working already in Colchester when, on his coming of age (21) his name appeared on the 1801 tax returns as owner of one of the best sites for a grocer and tea dealer in Colchester; the double fronted shop, 31 and 32, High Street, at the corner of Pelhams Lane in the parish of St. Runwald, with a rateable value of forty pounds a year (today occupied by Burtons, the tailors). Hard work and business ability made this an excellent investment for whoever made it possible for William Burgess to own this business; on the 9th of June 1801, his position as a leading burgess of the town was further established by his marriage to the twenty year old Elizabeth, daughter of the breeches-maker Robert Davis who had lived some years in the Parish of Saint Nicholas and kept a shop rated at seven pounds.

There were no children of this marriage, but the shop made William Burgess prosperous and well known and he became one of the group of enthusiastic evangelicals that attended Saint Peter's church. In spite of the 1842 fire, this church has changed little. The building is large without chancel or choir stalls, but with a large organ at the west end of the large raked gallery on three sides of the church. Today, as in the beginning of the nineteenth century in most churches, the choir still sits in the gallery at the back of the church. The size of the building, seating about 1,500, the structural emphasis on the pulpit rather than on the altar and the impassioned oratory of the curate, the Reverend John Bull B.A. made Saint Peter's church the inevitable centre of the auxiliary branch of the Colchester and East Essex British and Foreign Bible Society, supported by both evangelicals of the Church of England and Non-Conformists.

In 1804, to take the Bible to the people of the world translated into their own languages, the British and Foreign Bible Society had been founded in London, in spite of the objections of the high church party in the Anglican church, which maintained that the Society for the Propagation of Christian Knowledge, limited to members of the Church of England, was the rightful agent. By 1810, nine auxiliary branches already existed in various parts of the country, and in that year Colchester and the East Essex Auxiliary Bible Society was singled out as a test case to face the Anglican objection to the recruitment of protestant groups, from evangelical members of the Church of England to Quakers.

Abroad, England and her allies were fighting Napoleon; at home a battle raged between evangelicals and high churchmen over the right of Colchester to create an auxiliary branch; the defeat of Colchester would mean the dissolution of the British and Foreign Bible Society. In 1811, Colchester took the initiative and invited Randolph, the bishop of London and a high churchman, to become one of its vice-presidents, a reasonable request because Essex was part of the London diocese. But the invitation to Christopher Wordsworth, the domestic chaplain to the archbishop of Canterbury, and an avowed opponent of the Evangelicals, was a real challenge. Like Randolph, Wordsworth refused, but went further and published a bitter pamphlet about 'the sheep stealing zeal of the British and Foreign Bible Society'. However, the Evangelicals scored a great victory in Parliament, when in 1811 Lord Sidmouth's bill to restrict non-conformist itinerant preaching was defeated. At Cambridge university, the master of Queen's College led the evangelical cause. The growth of support for the British and Foreign Bible Society increased, and in 1812 Nicholas Vansittart, chancellor of the exchequer, accepted the invitation of the Colchester and East Essex Society to join its imposing list of vice-presidents. In 1813, the High Church party gave up the fight.

The first general meeting was held on the 9th October 1810, at the Moot Hall with the mayor of Colchester, Mr. F. Smythies in the chair. The structure of the organisation was simple and efficient; subscribers to the Colchester and East Essex Auxiliary Bible Association included individuals, an increasing number of Bible Associations of which Kirby le Soken (1814) was one of the first, Ladies' Associations which began in Colchester in 1813 with six hundred members paying one penny a week. From Colchester, a sum was sent annually to headquarters in Earlham Street, London, with a request for a certain sum to be spent on Bibles to be forwarded to Colchester to its depository, where they were sold at a reduced price; the balance was to be used by the parent society for its work. Thus in 1815 William Burgess sent £850, with the request that half the sum should be spent on Bibles and Testaments. There annual sums grew, as the Colchester organisation spread and legacies became a common feature. By the 1830's this enthusiastic chief secretary, by then Vicar and Commissary of the Sokens of Thorpe, Kirby and Walton, had organised the division of many parishes into districts for the organised sale and discussion of *The Bible* and Bibles were distributed to groups created by events both at home and abroad.

1814   Dutch Bibles to Captain Schewe of Amsterdam.

1816   Dutch Bibles to Dutch fishermen at Yarmouth.

1822   Preventive waterguard service stationed in the Martello Towers (including Walton and Great Clacton) and other places along the coast.

Colchester was for the Sokens not only the postal and main marketing town, but farmers sent their children to the small private boarding schools for girls as well as boys, and many went to learn a trade, including in 1810 Henry Baker apprenticed to a Colchester cabinet-maker. There he was invited by a young woman working in the same shop to join a few of the congregation at St. Peter's church at a prayer meeting early on Sunday morning before going to the service at church to hear Mr. Bull preach where, as Henry Baker explains in a letter, "I soon heard of Him I had need of." As a result, a lasting friendship grew up between Henry Baker and William Burgess. According to his letter to the Church Missionary Society dated 8th April, 1814, Henry was persecuted by his family for his religious views, and whether this was to poison the future relationship between his half brother Samuel Baker and William Burgess is difficult to determine. Certainly Henry Baker and all his family frequented William Burgess' vicarage at Thorpe-le-Soken and his house in North Street, Colchester rented by their mutual friend, Mr. Newell.

Encouraged by William Burgess, Henry Baker applied to the Church Missionary Society and finally sailed for Travancore in south India at the end of 1817. During this period, Burgess added zeal for overseas missions to his work for the British and Foreign Bible Society and in 1816 became founder secretary of the

Colchester and East Essex Church Missionary Association. Following the evangelical practice of purchasing advowsons to give them the right of making nominations of suitable clergy, in 1816 William Burgess bought the advowson of the Sokens of Kirby, Walton and Thorpe from the Reverend Thomas Scott, lord of the manor and patron of the living.

The early education and apprenticeship of William Burgess remain untraced, and his church accounts of the future were to be drawn up as only a successful businessman knows how, but education for the priesthood meant withdrawal from business. For three years Burgess lived at Littlebury, Essex, and studied in the household of the Rev. Henry Bull while the shop in Colchester was supervised by his wife Elizabeth. Then on Sunday, 16th November 1817, the following statement was sent from Littlebury church to the Bishop of Norwich:

"Whereas William Burgess of this Parish intends to offer himself a candidate for the holy order of Deacons at the ensuing ordination to be held by the Right Reverend the Lord Bishop of Norwich at Norwich on the sixteenth day of November; this is to give notice that if any Person can show sufficient Cause, just Impediment or notable Crime, for which the said William Burgess ought not to be admitted to that Holy Order, he may now declare the same, or give notice thereof by letter to the Bishop of Norwich."

The above notice was publicly read in the parish church of Littlebury in the County of Essex during the Time of Divine Service on Sunday, the 2nd day, Thursday the 6th day and Sunday the 9th day of November and no objections were made.

Henry Bull   Vicar.
Witnesses   Geo. Wilford   Churchwarden and
Nath. Robinson Principal Inhabitant.

This was accompanied by the birth certificate obtained in 1797 together with a letter — testimonial maintaining that "the said William Burgess, having been personally known to us for the Space of Three Years last past, hath during that time lived piously, soberly and honestly, and hath diligently applied himself to his studies" and signed by John Bull, rector of Tattingstone, Joseph Julian, rector of Hasketon and Edward Griffin, rector of St. Stephens, Ipswich. On 26th November 1817, William Burgess, ordained deacon, became curate of Tattingstone and priest on 30th November 1818, but parish registers show him as performing one office only, a baptism. The shop in Colchester was let and to complete his qualifications, in June 1818 he became a sizar (poor scholar) of the evangelical Queen's College, Cambridge, matriculated in 1817 and obtained his degree of Bachelor of Divinity in 1828, under the Act of Elizabeth I which gave the right to graduate to members of the clergy after a ten year registration. In 1819, he became curate of Mount Bures near Colchester and remained there until the living of the Sokens became vacant with the death of its vicar, the Reverend J. Stoney. During this last period, William Burgess toured frequently on behalf of the British and Foreign Bible Society, especially in East Anglia and was insistent that the London headquarters provide a good programme for Colchester which by 1823 had seven branch societies and twenty six Bible Associations. Their zeal is described in a letter from the Reverend Samuel Banks to headquarters dated 8th October 1839 and referring to their annual general meeting held usually in October at the full moon to make travelling easier:

"I have a dread of Colchester, they are so determined to get everything out of a man that I feel I should not have enough for them. I had two meetings and a sermon there last year and I thought that was pretty well, but two meetings and two sermons in three days on the same subject is really very terrifying."

On the 24th January 1823 William Burgess, now aged forty three, was admitted and instituted under his own patronage by William, Bishop of London, as vicar of the Sokens of Kirby, Walton and Thorpe and preached his first two sermons at Thorpe church on Sunday, February 2nd 1823 in the morning and afternoon services. These were published in the following April "to afford an opportunity to those who were not present, of judging of the views he entertains on the grand subject of his own ministrations — the Preaching of the Gospel; and of knowing the expectations which he considers himself scripturally entitled to entertain from his people in general." In these he explained that he regarded himself as the organ of the people in devotional exercises, leading them into actual service and with social links subordinated to preaching the Gospel. The Holy Spirit gave him the authority to "reprove and rebuke" as well as "to exhort". In the second sermon he maintained that a minister of Christ is warranted to expect from his people "Obedience to Ministerial Authority and Submission to Ministerial Instruction" for "If we point out to you what we consider erroneous, either in doctrine or in practice, remember it is because we watch for your souls." The vicar's feeling of responsibility was emphasised by a summary of his own duties which included visiting the sick, teaching and discussion. During 1823, Burgess wrote two letters only to Bible House because parochial affairs took up most of his time.

In 1823 William Burgess worked hard to restore the activities of the Commissary Court which had deteriorated under his predecessors and to create some kind of order in the business and legacies to the three parishes, including Doctor Avery's charity in Kirby which had been allowed to lapse. On February 19th and 20th, a month after his institution, "William Burgess, Vicar of the consolidated Vicarage of Kirby le Soken, Walton le Soken and Thorpe le Soken, petitioned the House of Lords and House of Commons respectively for the right to issue Marriage Licenses enjoyed by the predecessors of your petitioner . . . from time immemorial, among other rights and privileges of their Court . . . for all marriages within the said Liberty now made invalid by 'the late Marriage Act'; on October 6th, the petition proved successful."

Letters patent were granted by the lord of the manor, the Reverend Thomas Scott appointing William Burgess who took the oath:

"I, William Burgess, do swear that I will to the utmost of my understanding deal uprightly and justly in my Office of Commissary or Official Principal and Vicar General within the Peculiar Jurisdiction of the Sokens in the County of Essex without respect of favour or reward, so help me God."

On October 20th, the churchwardens of the three parishes were summoned to appear at a general Commissary Court in Thorpe church "on Monday, the 27th of October, 1823 between the hours of ten and twelve in the forenoon of the same day, then and there to make and exhibit their Bills of Presentment, giving notice in the meantime to the Churchwardens Elect, also to appear to be admitted and sworn into Office." At this first court attended by the churchwardens of Kirby le Soken, where the farmers Mr. Benjamin Barton of Horsey Island and Mr. Barnabas Wilson made their report and the newly elected Mr. Richard Stone of Willow Farm and Frinton Hall was sworn in, William Burgess emphasised that he intended "to support the last surviving privilege, among many, which this district once enjoyed". Churchwardens were reminded that they were "Officers instituted to protect the Edifice of the Church, to superintend the Ceremonies of Public Worship, to promote the observance of Religious Duties, to form and execute Parochial Regulations, and to become, as occasion may require, the representatives of the Body of the Parish". As guardians of public morals the Church entrusted them 'with the charge of correcting the profane and vicious lives of others'; thus to inspect public houses, prevent corrupting theatrical performances especially at the annual fairs which attract 'numbers of the idle and dissolute of both sexes.' To the end of his life in 1862, William Burgess resisted archdeacon's visitation, insisting on the Soken right to make parochial returns direct to the bishop.

Once established, the vicar worked hard to bring education to his parishioners. Through Sunday schools in particular, many children learned to read and *The Bible* or *New Testament* was the only book available; the cost of the cheapest Bible (bound in calf) to the East Essex Auxiliary Bible Society was 4s. 4d. (22p) and sold at the reduced price of 3s. 3d. (16p). William Burgess spent £228. 14. 2. (£228.70) in building schools for Thorpe and Kirby le Soken, with Kirby School in the churchyard. However, as he explained in a return to the Bishop of London in 1830, day school was impossible where the children were needed to work in the fields; so, although the fashionable watering place Walton already owned a well attended day school, both Thorpe and Kirby used their newly built school on Sundays only until the 1850's.

As he had stated in his first sermon, William Burgess felt responsible for the welfare of his parishioners, and insisted on not only the repair and extension of seating in the three churches to provide for "the poor who have an equal right to a resting place with the rich"; but also on the removal of nuisances from the church and churchyard, and in 1831 exhorted his churchwardens to insist on measures for cleanliness and proper ventilation to prevent the spread of disease. A relentless war was waged on those who profaned the Sabbath whether by drinking in a beer shop, running coaches from Colchester to Walton, making trips from Walton Harbour by pleasure steamer or operating windmills. He attacked Roman Catholics, ceremonial in the Church of England, disturbance of the social order, slavery 'that pernicious system', the admission of Jews to Parliament, Divorce, the smuggling traffic in Opium by English traders in China, the abolition of the Church Rate and mourned the drift of agricultural workers to the towns so that the population of Kirby declined by 127 between 1851 and 1861.

At the Commissary Court of October 29th 1827 he warned his churchwardens that he would not "sanction the appropriating to an individual more room than he really wants, nor the appropriating of pews to Houses in perpetuity; they do not, nor ever can become private property". The matter of the rebuilding of Kirby church was to become an explosive issue between the Reverend William Burgess and Mr Samuel Baker of Birch Hall and Meers Farm.

APPENDIX TWO

CHURCH FEES
Within the Liberty and Peculiar Jurisdiction of the Sokens.

Accustomed Service Fees.

Marriages			Searching of Extract	
By License	10.	6.	from Register	2. 6.
By Banns	5.	0.		
Publication of			*Burials*	
Banns	1.	0.	In the Churchyard	
Certificate of do.	1.	0.	—grave service	2. 6.
Searching of Extract			In do. Church	
from Register	2.	6.	service	7. 6.
			Corpse carried to	
Baptisms and Churchings			any other place of	
			interment	2. 6.
Registering Baptism				
and Churching	1.	0.	Searching of Extract	
Baptisms on Weekdays	2.	6.	from Register	2. 6.

34

Extra Burial Fees

In the Churchyard					*In the Church*			
Vault, with 2 Coffins	5.	5.	0.	Do. on Head and foot stone		5.	0.	
Opening do.	2.	12.	6.	Burial Monument outside church	1.	1.	0.	
Single Brick Grave	1.	1.	0.	Do. large size	2.	2.	0.	
Opening do.		10.	6.					
Raised Tomb over vault with Iron railings	3.	13.	6.	Vault with 2 coffins	10.	10.	0.	
				Opening Do.	5.	5.	0.	
Do. without railings	2.	0.	0.	Single Brick Grave	5.	5.	0.	
Tomb or covering over single brick or other grave	1.	1.	0.	Opening do.	2.	12.	6.	
				Burial Monument	2.	2.	0.	
Head and foot stone 2 graves	1.	1.	0.	Do. large size	5.	5.	0.	
Do. and do. single grave		10.	6.	Do., Do., base on ground	10.	10.	0.	
Fresh inscription on Tomb		10.	6.	Marble or Stone over vault or brick grave	2.	2.	0.	
				Hatchment	2.	2.	0.	

Double fees in all the preceding cases for persons brought from other parishes.

CHAPTER THREE

Revolt and Reform

'Changes are both projected and contemplated, which would have startled our forefathers' (Rev. Wm. Burgess to Churchwardens, 23rd June, 1831.)

I THE TENDRING RIOTS

On 26th June, 1830, George IV died which resulted in a General Election and the issue of parliamentary reform became all important. By the time the elections were held for fourteen days from 6th August, revolution had broken out in France where, on 29th July Charles X abdicated; two weeks later, Louis Philippe was elected king of the French. These incidents sparked off a succession of national rebellions with demands for constitutional monarchy, and, as in the case of Belgium, independence. So the English elections took place in an atmosphere of great excitement. The unfair qualification for rural voters was obvious in Kirby le Soken where (apart from absentee landlords who were uninterested) only six voted on the Tendring husting at Chelmsford: Mr. Henry Blanchard of Horsey Island, three prosperous tenant farmers who held a small area of freehold land—John Dennis Daniels, Richard Stone and William Wilson, and John Gifford and James L. Webb who just qualified as voters on this forty shilling freeholder franchise. The strength of the demand for parliamentary reform is understandable in a system which gave none of the following the right to vote: Samuel Baker who paid 1/6 of the Kirby Rates and Robert Mumford of Kirby Hall, both tenant farmers; with Jeremiah Foaker of Sneating Hall who held his land by copyhold. While the Whig leaders, Lord Grey and Lord John Russell, with three elections between 1830 and 1832 and a confrontation with the

House of Lords, struggled to extend the franchise, Essex farmers watched the plight of the agricultural labourers with some anxiety.

Until rioting broke out, labourers throughout Essex had the sympathy of 'Members of Parliament, magistrates, clergymen, landowners, farmers . . . merchants and tradesmen without distinction of party.' A meeting in the middle of February called together by the high sheriff proved startlingly successful; and, under the leadership of Mr. Daniel Whittle Harvey, the radical member of parliament for Colchester, the gathering drew up a petition for presentation to Parliament. This drew attention to 'the Misery and Privations of the majority of the People' caused by the inadequacy of parliamentary representation, unequal taxation and the need for the commutation of tithe by act of parliament. In the spring of 1830, the *Kent and Essex Mercury* pursued the demands for parliamentary reform, and in its leader of 27th April, attacked the chairman of magistrates because he ignored the distress of the poor. 'When men cannot support themselves and their families by their own labour—and when Overseers of the Poor are compelled to refuse Relief, from the utter impossibility of collecting the Rates—the Pauper, has no other alternative than starvation or plunder.'

By 9th February, the number of unemployed poor throughout Essex was unprecedented 'due not only to the unpropitious state of the weather, but to the inability of the farmers from want of pecuniary resources, to employ them.' The Tendring Hundred was overpopulated: during the eighteenth century and until 1815, good soils and easy sea transport encouraged progressive farmers to live in the district, eager to use new methods; the agricultural boom brought in labourers, especially from Suffolk, but with the depression after 1815 came little alternative employment; migration to London was difficult because of the distance. By 1827, twenty labourers in Kirby were unemployed, and, with their families, supported by the poor rate paid by the farmers. The threshing machine aggravated the situation by depriving them of work during the winter: Samuel Baker owned a machine in his barn at Walton where he farmed 145 acres, but its use affected the Kirby 871 acres of Birch Hall, Meers Farm, Marsh Farm, Lane End, Skippers and Fishers. In spite of the Corn Law sliding scale of 1828 which taxed imported corn, using 73 shillings a quarter as the ceiling, in

December 1829, after three bad winters, a large amount of much needed grain was imported from the Baltic:—

Wheat	1.5 million	quarters
Barley	360,000	quarters
Oats	200,000	quarters

English farmers were criticised by the press for forcing on to the market cold and wet grain to economise on the expensive harvesting caused by bad weather of what was, in Essex, a reasonable crop.

The agricultural risings of 1830 spread from village to village over all the southern counties from Kent to Wiltshire and Dorset, throughout the eastern counties and a large part of the midlands, but without a formulated common programme: in the Soken area, on three successive days riots took place in Thorpe and Great Holland, Great Clacton and in Kirby and Walton in turn. They demanded from the church and landlords, a remission of tithes and a general lowering of rents for the farmers who would then be able to pay them higher wages. Rioting broke out in Kent at the beginning of November, but *The Kent and Essex Mercury* warned its readers that the swearing in of Special Constables was unwise while Essex remained peaceful. In less than a week, the Tendring riots broke out. On the 6th of December, Richard Stone of Kirby together with representatives of Little Bromley, Lawford, Walton and Little Clacton (five representatives required by law) swore before the justices of the peace 'that tumult or riot is likely to take place and may be reasonably apprehended within the Division or Hundred of Tendring . . . And they therefore pray that a sufficient number of Special Constables may be appointed for the preservation of the Peace within the said Division or Hundred'. On the following day, a notice displayed at the petty sessions of Maningtree arranged for the swearing-in of Special Constables to deal with the illegal assemblies of labourers and demanded that 'the Ringleaders were to be apprehended if the Rioters refuse to state their grievances to the Magistrate and to disperse'. Forty-four Kirby inhabitants with two from the tiny village of Frinton were sworn in on 7th December and equipped with truncheons in their capacity as mounted Special Constables—too late for the serious risings in Great Clacton and Thorpe.

For many rioters from Kirby and Great Clacton, hatred of the threshing machine was coupled by a hostility towards the preventive men, for smuggling was profitable business in the creeks and small ports of the area. Beer shops were usually the smugglers' headquarters, and the position of Robert Button's premises at Kirby Cross provided an ideal meeting place at the crossroads linking Walton, Kirby, Thorpe, Great Clacton and Great Holland and so inland to Colchester. The sanction of the use of preventive men to suppress the riots by the government, was most unpopular, and the only real threat of bloodshed by the rioters of Kirby le Soken was made against the six customs' officers guarding the machine at Walton Ashes. Used to co-operation under dangerous conditions, the Kirby leaders skilfully organised their machine—breaking with the greatest possible (if sometimes unwilling) support, against two farmers only: Samuel Baker employing the most labour and Samuel Wilson who sought the help of the preventive; neither rick-burning nor personal assault took place, as in other areas.

Early in the morning of Wednesday, 8th December, Samuel Baker Junior with Benjamin Ruffles, a farm labourer, were ploughing at Marsh Farm overlooking the Saltings. At about 7.30 a.m. they saw a group of forty or fifty labourers, armed with sticks and led by John Phipps, coming towards them. When the men reached Ruffles, they ordered him to join them and when he refused, closed in with their cudgels raised. The young Mr. Baker protested, only to be told that, if he interfered, they were prepared to take him with them, as well as his labourer whom they were prepared to carry if necessary. Then they made their object plain: the threshing machine of Mr. Samuel Baker in Walton Barn and that of Mr. Samuel Wilson at Walton Ashes were to be broken up.

Samuel Wilson, on hearing of the rioters' intention, rode to meet them and at about 9.30 found the mob, now about 150 strong, at Kents Hill (near the Kirby/Thorpe border). Thomas Grant, labourer of Kirby, told Wilson to go home because they were coming to break his machine. Angrily, Wilson retorted that the machine was not in their Parish and that his own men were quite satisfied, but the ringleaders refused to listen. Wilson warned the mob that he had the preventive men guarding his machines and was frightened at the angry reaction. Grant laughed and said that they 'would have blood for blood' and could easily destroy the hated officers. Now thoroughly alarmed, Wilson rode to seek help from the Kirby Special Constables and farmers who had arranged a meeting in the afternoon opposite the Church. When riding through Kirby le Soken on his way to his farm, Walton Ashes, once again Wilson met the rioters, who, by this time were in an ugly mood. They surged into the blacksmith's shop near the church and looted the sledge hammers and all that they could lay hands on. Because he realised the danger now that the labourers were armed, the farmer rode through the rioters 'to tell the Preventive Men they had better go because of the determined mob'. In the early afternoon, the rioters (by this time numbering over 200) assembled at Kirby Cross outside the beer shop, ready for the march along the road to Walton. There they were found by Mr. Samuel Baker (accompanied by one of his labourers) who challenged them. In reply to his questions, they told him that 'their intention was to break the Machinery and demand more wages'. The farmer protested and warned them that they had better not go breaking machines and that he 'would never work it any more if they would let it alone'. The ringleaders swore and told him that they could not trust his word. In his statement, Baker continued:—

> 'I asked them how they would like me to go into their yard and cut up their cabbages, trees and bushes. I said I might as well lose my life as my property; I should protect it as long as I could'.

The men refused to listen and began their march along what is now Frinton Road 'to the Barn a short distance from the Farm (Meers Farm) in which was the Machine'. While the labourers marched along the road Mr. Baker rode across the fields and arrived first at the Barn Yard Gate where he awaited the rioters. When they were refused entry by the gate, 'they jumped over the Northern Wall', to reach the barn door against which Baker now stood refusing to unlock it, and face to face with one of the rioters wielding a pickaxe and shouting that they would break down the door. On the advice of the farm labourer, Abraham Carrington, who had remained at his side throughout the day, Samuel Baker finally unlocked the Barn door and, according to his account:—

> 'Draper with some others shoved me backwards from the barn door they rent the lock off opened the door and rushed into the barn and broke the Machine all to pieces. The

Prisoner Phipps broke the Machine and was one of the first and most active.'

Once they had achieved their first objective, the elated rioters marched along the road (now Elm Tree Avenue) to Walton Ashes and arrived just before two o'clock. Samuel Wilson, who had sent away the preventive men, stood at the gate. At the command of Phipps they forced Wilson's labourers to join them, and, armed with the looted sledge hammers and pickaxes, surrounded the farmer. At the trial Wilson stated:—

'Davey shoved me against the Gate and he pulled the Gate open and the mob ran to the cart-lodge where part of the Machine was . . . I had placed carts against the Machine but they pulled them out and got at the Machine, which they brought into the Yard and hammered it to pieces.'

John Phipps soon realised that parts of the machine were missing and demanded the key to the barn. When Wilson told him that the key had been sent away, one of the mob climbed through a small window by using a long ladder and opened the doors from the inside. The men dragged out the machine parts and broke them up, watched helplessly by Mr. Samuel Wilson and a passing farmer, Mr. John Fisher of Kirby.

Once the rioters had destroyed the machines of Messrs Baker and Wilson, they turned to their final objective of gaining an increase in wages. Led by John Phipps, they marched towards the centre of Kirby where the farmers were holding their meeting opposite the Church. The mob, between two and three hundred strong, surrounded the farmers. Phipps, with a sledge hammer in one hand and a paper in the other, approached Mr. Samuel Baker and handed him the paper containing the men's demands which was passed on to Mr. Robert Mumford of Kirby Hall. As a result of this confrontation, the assembled farmers agreed to the wages demanded: two shillings a day and seven shillings a week for unemployed single men. Once their objectives were achieved, the rioters of Kirby le Soken dispersed.

To restore order within the Tendring Hundred, a stronger force than special constables was needed. Two days earlier, the constable of Thorpe was refused military assistance by the commandant of the Harwich station, but reminded that the help of the Walton coastguards under the command of Lieutenant Jeffries was available; this help was sought by Thomas Bundock, butcher, the constable of Kirby le Soken after taking part in the general round-up of rioters organised by the meeting of special constables on Tendring Heath on 9th December. Thomas Bundock escorted two groups to Chelmsford for trial, and finally John Phipps on his own. The first group of seven including George Davey, the Grant brothers (Thomas, James and John) and William Jeffries, were doubtless put in the cage before being escorted to the petty sessions at Maningtree and thence to Springfield gaol, Chelmsford to await trial (within a week) at the assizes after grand jury proceedings.

On this first occasion, with the whole of Tendring in a state of unrest, the seven prisoners were escorted by ten guards including Robert Mumford, Samuel Baker Junior, John Gifford, the builder, Thomas Bundock and Lieutenant Jeffries with his men; as a safeguard, 'a rescue being apprehended' six, including the Thorpe Officer of Excise, formed an additional escort as far as Colchester. The second group of fourteen (mostly from Great Clacton), including Samuel Draper and Robert Davey of Kirby was escorted from Thorpe petty sessions to Chelmsford by Thomas Bundock, Lieutenant Jeffries, the constable of Thorpe and five others for the quarter sessions on Tuesday, January 4th, 1831; John Phipps, the last to be rounded up, was tried with this group. Those who took part in the Kirby riots were prosecuted by Mr. Samuel Wilson. Although Mr. Samuel Baker made a sworn statement at the petty sessions, supported by those of Benjamin Ruffles and Abraham Carrington, indicting John Phipps and Robert Keeble ('late of Walton') 'for having broken a Machine belonging to Mr. Samuel Baker', no evidence was offered and the two men were acquitted of this charge. (Samuel Baker was to behave in a similar fashion when summoned three times to the Commissary Court to produce evidence against the rebuilding of Kirby church in 1832).

Nationally, the sentences were savage: nine were hanged, 457 transported and as many imprisoned; and this with the use of troops in some areas. But of the Kirby mob of 200 to 300, nine only were arrested. All were sentenced to transportation to Van Dieman's Land: Thomas and James Grant with George Davey for fourteen years, the others for seven. After being convicted, the prisoners were sent to await transportation in the *York* and *Leviathan* hulks at Portsmouth and sailed for Hobart in the *Eliza II* on 6th February, 1831 and in *The Proteus* on 11th April, 1831. The twenty year old John Phipps, however, was not among those transported, nor has any record been found of his whereabouts after he was sentenced.

The clerk of the peace of the Tendring Hundred in a letter to the Home Secretary, Lord Melbourne, summed up the situation:—

'Two fires occurred in this Hundred and twelve Threshing Machines have been destroyed and numerous threatening letters circulated. About fifty rioters were apprehended, have been tried at the Assizes and all found Guilty . . . We trust that Order is now restored. Our endeavours were greatly aided by the Promptitude and Energy of Lieutenant Jeffries of the Coast Guard at Walton and his Division as well as by the Chief Constable and mounted Constabulary Force'.

Rewards for the apprehension of machine breakers were paid to 69 persons in the Hundred (sums varying between £5 and £85) and totalled £1,950. Farmers received compensation for destroyed threshing machines: Samuel Wilson claimed £45 and was paid £34.16.6; Samuel Baker's valuation of £50 was met by £18.18. Helped by a succession of good harvests, labourers' wages were increased, and the use of threshing machines declined until about 1843. Politically, the revolts highlighted the need for parliamentary reform to create a middle class parliament powerful enough to bring up to date game laws, payment of tithe and the Poor Law.

The Parliamentary Reform Bill which became law on 4th June, 1832 gave the vote to the £10 copyholder and £50 leaseholder and tenant-at-will—in addition to the 40 shilling freeholder. For the first time, parish overseers dealt with the registration of voters and the Sokens had a husting at Thorpe on which 25 of the 28 registered voters of Kirby voted on 21st and 22nd December, 1832 for two candidates to represent Essex. Throughout Britain, the events of 1830 to 1832 emphasised the problems created by growing industrialisation at loggerheads with centuries of tradition: payment of tithe, poverty, disorder and the cholera epidemic of 1831. For Kirby le Soken as part of rural England, the reform parliament of January 1833 marked the beginning of a new era which was reflected in the rebuilding of its church.

II THE REBUILDING OF THE PARISH CHURCH

In 1830, the outside of the Parish Church of Kirby le Soken looked much as the church of Saint Michael does today in spite of the 1833 major rebuilding. The square tower of flint stood at the west end with the main building made of septaria, 'commonly called Rolk or Shore Stones', occasionally repaired with brick and supported by brick buttresses. Inside, the church was fifty feet long, forty feet wide and eighteen feet high, with what looked like an extension on the south side forming a south aisle, with pews on each side; the congregation entered by the north porch. At the west end, across the high arch leading to the tower, was a small gallery, twenty-two feet wide, approached by a staircase on the north side of the interior of the tower; on its south side a narrow stone spiral staircase led to the belfry in which hung five bells. The chancel contained, not the choir stalls, but three large box pews; singers and instrumentalists sat in the gallery.

This church provided problems in 1830. Not only was the building dilapidated, but inhabitants paying tithe occupied large family pews which together seated 206 persons leaving 85 free places on benches in a village of 972 inhabitants. The most elaborate pew was linked to Meers Farm by a faculty granted on the first of April 1726 and the tenant, Samuel Baker, jealously maintained his rights and kept his pew in good repair. Finally, at the back of the church, was the family tomb of John King (eleven feet by twelve feet) in the north-west corner and on the south side, an over-large vestry (21 feet by 12 feet); together the two structures prevented the use of a quarter of the building for seating purposes. So the Reverend William Burgess, vicar and commissary of the Sokens, was determined that not only was Kirby parish church to be completely repaired, but seating provided for every man, woman and child in the parish.

When holding the annual Commissary Court to hear the annual report of the outgoing churchwardens and for the citation of the new churchwardens of Kirby, Thorpe and Walton, William Burgess made his wishes known from 1825, pointing out that the repair of all three churches was imperative, for no longer 'could the events of the preceding years' (the war against France 1793 to 1815) be pleaded as an excuse and that the poor had 'an equal right to have a resting place with the rich' if they were 'to remain steadfast in the faith'. He warned the churchwardens in 1825, that the removal of nuisances and obstructions 'unbecoming to the Sanctity of the Church or Churchyard' was part of their duty, and if they failed to carry this out, he was prepared to seek 'the interposition of Ecclesiastical authority'. Money for this purpose must be raised by a separate rate and did not form part of the poor rate. Two years later, on 29th October, 1827, after congratulating the Thorpe churchwardens on the rebuilding of their church, the vicar made the legal position quite clear: the church rate must be raised at a parish vestry meeting; the Commissary or Ordinary had the right to hold a special court to summon members of the opposition to state their case; the chancel was the financial responsibility of the Landlord collecting the great tithe; seats were 'not to be annexed or appropriated to any estate' nor any houses as such, so that pews 'do not, nor ever can, become private property'; and the distribution of seats remains with the Ordinary. Addressing the churchwardens of Kirby, in particular, William Burgess said that he relied on their best exertions to place it in a proper state of repair with 'sufficient for the comfortable accommodation of the parishioners'.

In June 1828 Benjamin Barton of Horsey Island, vicar's warden for over fifty years, died in office, aged eighty five. This event provided William Burgess with two powerful allies in the parish: the wealthy gentleman, Jeremiah Foaker, copyhold occupier of Sneating Hall became vicar's warden until he left the parish in 1850 and Henry Blanchard acquired Horsey Island and was to prove both generous and influential. Inevitably, therefore, at the court in June 1830, William Burgess addressed the Kirby wardens even more forcibly, saying that 'rebuilding and additional accommodation was being impeded by every obstacle, which apathy and indifference can suggest and a parsimonious withholding of the means, without any regard to the necessary consequences that will ensue'. In 1828, two builders, Samuel Baker's brother-in-law, Robert Large of Great Clacton and Joseph Salmon of Beaumont cum Moze, had informed the churchwardens that any attempt to shore up the south wall would result in the roof falling in, and were asked to make a final report to the Kirby vestry meeting of April 4th, 1831; the minutes recorded that £1,000 would be needed for the repairs. But in May, to make sure of the necessity of large scale repairs, William Burgess called in an experienced surveyor without building interests, to examine the whole structure and to estimate the cost of repairs and increased seating accommodation.

Mr. Joseph Parkins of Colchester reported that the roof had given way because the principal timbers were rotten, so that the south wall and buttresses were forced out; the situation was worsened by graves dug near the foundations, making the interior row of pillars and the arches with buttresses fourteen inches out of upright. The walls were built principally of shore stone, but the mortar that held them together had lost its strength, leaving a number 'of Cracks and Breaches' which made it useless to preserve them. The floor had sunk below the level of the church so that not only the south side, but pews, pulpit and desk were rotten. The flint tower was cracked and the oak joists that supported the bells and frame were dangerous because some were completely rotten at the ends close to the walls. Most window frames and louvre boards were rotten and partly 'gone' so that the rain came in; and the north porch was dilapidated. Mr. Parkins estimated the cost of rebuilding and repairing to be £1,009.17.9, and his suggestions were finally adopted.

It was necessary to take off the roof, demolish the south wall up to the chancel and the tower respectively 'together with all Interior Pillars and Arches and the Buttresses by which they are now supported', and then to use these materials to help rebuild all four walls eighteen inches higher with windows of crown glass set in iron frames. The repaired structure was covered by a substantial tiled roof supported by rafters and the floor was raised 22 inches. To safeguard the repairs as well as to increase seating accommodation by 216, the existing pews were demolished and at the west end, the gallery, vestry and John King's tomb were taken down. Two family vaults were sealed: a stone tablet on the south wall commemorates the King family and the dedication of the Savage vault is visible on the outer wall. Yellow deal was used for all the woodwork: the church was repewed and one 'substantial' gallery constructed at the west end extending from the north to south wall, 'in length 40 feet and in depth 12 feet 6 inches', clearing the main body of the church by eight feet. A new vestry room (today partly occupied by the organ) was built on to the south east corner, with an entrance into the chancel and its outer door leading into the churchyard. In the tower a strong oak bearer 12 inches by 10 inches supported the ends of the joist in the belfry with an iron bolt through the walls at each end; a new bell frame, louvre boards in the belfry and a new floor and joist for the ringers were installed. The repaired north porch was given a new door into the church.

Seating was completely reorganised. The Reverend William Burgess objected to high box pews into which the owners could lock themselves, so the new pews rose 3 feet 9 inches from the floor, each fitted with a bookshelf and a hat rail under the seat and the pew door fastened with a neat brass button. The pews were arranged with four in the chancel (two on each side facing each other) and four pews on its north corner faced eight on the south. The new pulpit was moved to the corner of the south side and at its base, was a pew each for the vicar and his curate, the Reverend Warwell Fenn. Free seating was provided by eight free benches in the north west corner of the church (made with framed backs and cut elbows), six long free benches at the back of the centre and south side raised on a platform under the gallery, together with 110 in the gallery itself; in the rest of the building were the box pews facing the Communion Table at the east end. Further free seating was provided by movable double benches in the north aisle.

The opposition to the rebuilding of the parish church, centred in Mr. Samuel Baker of Birch Hall and Meers Farm, came at a time of national and local unrest. Although the Tendring riots of farm labourers were over and the offenders sentenced, England was in the throes of the Parliamentary Reform Bill agitation and by 1831, suffering from a cholera epidemic, regarded by William Burgess as God's punishment for the sin and apathy of its people. At the Commissary Court of June 1832, the churchwardens, Messrs Jeremiah Foaker of Sneating Hall and William George Clark Warner of Devereux Farm, formally presented documents requesting a licence and faculty for rebuilding; the expenses were to be covered by:— £300 from the Incorporated Society for Promoting the Enlarging, Building and Repairing of Churches, the promise of £205 from friends and £300 to be raised by a three years' rate of one shilling in the pound; the balance of £200 the churchwardens hoped to raise by voluntary contributions. The

47

citation (details of the proposal) was publicly displayed in the church and, at the Court of 3rd July, parishioners were called to make their objections. Samuel Baker did not appear, but sent a written protest by Jeremiah Foaker, so a special court was arranged on 27th July for his attendance. This time Samuel Baker again failed to attend, but sent a list of objections: the Commissary Court was illegal, the enlargement and repair of the church unnecessary, parishioners had little fair discussion because they had been overwhelmed by William Burgess in the chair and his pew in the church was legally part of the messuage of Meers Farm. Although in a letter to the vicar, legal opinion in London described Baker as a litigious character who would be troublesome in the business' and advised Burgess to ignore him, on 3rd August, 'for the sake of peace and goodwill', Samuel was summoned for a third hearing. Again he failed to appear and sent a written protest by Richard Stone of Frinton Hall and Willow Farm who disassociated himself from the contents. Three times Samuel Baker had been given the opportunity to protest in the Commissary's court and, for the two last occasions, a special summons from the court's official apparitor (summoner), was delivered to Birch Hall, Samuel Baker's main residence. For over a year the repairs had been delayed, but on 25th August, William Burgess, Vicar and Commissary of the Sokens, granted to 'Jeremiah Foaker and William George Clark Warner our Licence and Faculty for Repairing and Enlarging the said Church'.

But Samuel Baker was not yet defeated. Already in 1831, he had drawn up a petition which, according to Burgess's written statement to the Incorporated Society, he 'sent round for signatures to such tradesmen as were under his influence, accompanied by a threat that if they did not sign it, he would remove his work from them, and under this threat it was signed in most instances, and by several others, without knowledge of its contents, and solely to avoid offending Mr. Baker'. When, in spite of all his protests, the faculty for repairing the church was granted, in October 1832 Samuel sent a petition signed mostly by tradesmen of Lower Kirby, asking the Incorporated Society for Promoting the Enlarging, Building and Repairing of Churches to withdraw the promised grant of £300, claiming that the rate would 'bear hard upon the industrious and meritorious class of Ratepayers' and (quite accurately) that he paid 1/6th of the parish rates. The list of twenty signatories is interesting: shopkeeper, tailor, wheelwright, blacksmith, gardener, maltster, shoemaker, the keepers of the 'Ship' and 'Red Lion' inns and of the beer house at Kirby Cross; several small farmers and a widow related to him by marriage. Upon receipt of a copy of this petition William Burgess forwarded a full statement to the Incorporated Society and in letters dated 29th November, 1832 to both Samuel Baker and the vicar, expressed its satisfaction with the arrangements made. Baker's objections ceased, diverted perhaps by the excitement of voting on the Thorpe Husting on December 21 and 22 for the first time.

The builder, Mr. Joseph Salmon of Beaumont, whose tender of £1,019.7.00 was accepted, agreed to work under the direction of the surveyor and to farm out brickwork to the village builder, John Gifford; the church was to be ready for divine service six months from the beginning of the work, which had to await the spring. So on Sunday, April 14th, 1833, the Reverend William Burgess conducted the last service in the old church and in his sermon compared the parishioners with the Jews returning from the Babylonian captivity who had neglected to rebuild the temple until God had shown his anger by destroying their harvest. But God had been merciful to Kirby, giving its inhabitants an abundant harvest and keeping them free from cholera; as a thank offering for life, the members of the congregation were urged 'to put into the Plate the price of a Coffin'. During the six months schedule, services were to be held in the Kirby schoolroom in addition to the rebuilt churches of Thorpe and Walton.

The rebuilt church of Kirby le Soken 'not named after any saint' stood in a large churchyard, 'well fenced and decently kept' by a ditch and quickset hedge. A latched gate opened from the road to the gravel paths and a water trough was maintained outside it at parish expense for worshippers' horses. On the square flint tower, a steeple supported a gilded weathervane and the uncluttered interior with nearly six hundred sittings was plastered and painted white with the stone steps regularly whitened with hearthstone. Much of the chancel decoration completed in 1818 preserved its appearance until the 1940's. Four panels of lead, weighing a total of over three hundredweight, were fixed to the wall above eye-level, two on each side of the Communion Table: as they faced east, in gilded lettering on a black background worshippers saw the Ten Commandments and the Lord's Prayer on the north side and on the south, the creed. The words 'My Flesh is Meat Indeed' and 'My Blood is Drink Indeed' were painted in a type of ornamental scroll formation on the east wall, high above the lettered panels. The injunction 'Reverence My Sanctuary' decorated the nave side of the chancel arch in large gothic lettering. Furnishings included the Communion Table with candles and new hangings, the pulpit with its sounding board on the south corner of the nave and chancel, the reading desk with its Bible but the font, described as 'adequate' by the churchwardens in 1834 was later severely criticised by church authorities. The royal coat of arms decorated the front of the new west gallery.

Ready for Sunday, 20th October, 1833, the new pews, allowing 18 inches for an adult, were allocated by William Burgess and the churchwardens. Unfortunately, most of the records of Kirby parish church were destroyed in a private house during the Second World War by a V2, so this seating plan for 507 sittings in 'Kirby New Church' is unavailable. However, the 1827 plan for Thorpe church suggests the likely arrangements. Those that paid tithe sat in a family pew allocated, with the more important families in or near the chancel. However, families in the free seats were divided up according to age, sex and function. If, as we know from the surveyor's plan, the benches on the raised platform seated ninety children, we assume that the benches of the north west corner and the double seats in the north aisle were intended for the women: widows in the front of female servants and labourers' wives at the back. This puts male labourers in the gallery (with perhaps one pew allocated to the few men servants) on each side of the singers.

On Wednesday, 16th October, six months after the rebuilding was begun, the dedication service was held in Kirby new church, and the vicar rejoiced at 'the delightful sight of a large congregation assembled at the re-opening of the House of God'. On this historic occasion, the sermon was preached by the Reverend George Fiske, S.C.L. of Corpus Chisti College, Cambridge and the Anthems sung by male singers organised by Robert Mumford of Kirby Hall. At the 'First Sabbath Service', the Reverend William Burgess in his sermon based on Solomon's dedication of the Temple, took the opportunity of thanking for financial support, not only the Incorporated Society for £300, but the Bishop of London for £20, £100 from the owner of the great tithe (the late W. P. Honeywood Esq.) to cover repairs of the chancel, £100 from Mr. Henry Blanchard of Horsey Island and £200 from other friends. He went on to praise the churchwardens 'for their unremitting attention to the object in view, frequently under circumstances of considerable difficulty', and expressed his pleasure that no accidents had occurred 'either in taking down the old edifice or in the creation of the new'. Addressing those he termed 'Poorer Friends', he pointed out that they had special reason to be thankful because 'for them, and for their children attending our Sunday school, nearly all the increase of actual Sitting Room has been provided'.

So the third and last of the Soken churches was rebuilt and adequate seating was made available to the poor. Appropriately, among those joining in the thanksgiving was William Burgess's protegé and friend, the Reverend Henry Baker of the Church Missionary Society, home on leave with his wife and family from South India. Almost certainly, the dedication of Kirby new church marks the peak of the Reverend William Burgess's achievements.

CHAPTER FOUR

The Problem of the Poor

'Expectations are baffled and calculations are disappointed, and opinions are mistaken, and those who have thought themselves well skilled in human affairs are at a loss.''

(W. Burgess to Churchwardens 1851)

The period following the election of the 1832 Parliament was dominated by the problems of poverty and the maintenance of good order. However, in Kirby le Soken the elected parish surveyors of highways tried to solve parish road problems including that of straying animals. These were put into the pound on the common land on Quay Lane until the owner paid a shilling to regain his stock: sow, pigs, donkeys, sheep, lambs and, even occasionally, a pony. The traditional annual fairs were held on 26th July and another for lambs in August, but a real effort was made by responsible farmers to develop farming skills and to encourage long service by the establishment of the Tendring Hundred Agricultural Association (financed by the farmers) which held its first show at Thorpe on 1st June 1838. This included not only livestock and agricultural implements but also the labouring skills of ploughing and sheep shearing; prizes were also awarded for long service and good husbandry. The Reverend William Burgess and many local farmers and gentry encouraged thrift by voluntary contributions to set up the Tendring Hundred Provident and Benefit Society in 1837 to replace the Friendly Society of 1826. This supported men between fifteen and fifty years old who saved to help themselves in time of trouble: a scale beginning with a minimum payment of 3¾ pence (less than 2p) from the age of fifteen provided a weekly sickness benefit of two shillings, one shilling for unemployment and retirement at sixty-five and one pound at death.

The Tendring riots had provided a sharp lesson not only in the need for a professional police force, but also in a more sympathetic approach towards the needs of the labourers. The families of the rioters remained in Kirby and only once did the Guardians prove vindictive when they refused out relief to Elizabeth Grant, wife of James Grant transported for fourteen years, and told her to go with her child to the workhouse in October 1840. Following the pattern of the London police force, the 1839 County Police Act resulted in a meeting of the Essex justices who planned a police force of 115 including superintendents and appointed Captain John B. McHardy R.N., an ex coast guard who had taken a leading part in the suppression of the riots, to carry it out. The first police constable was appointed to Kirby (collar Number 170) in January 1857 and the force became finally established in the parish when First Class P.C. Benjamin Salmon served for thirty years at 21 shillings a week, finally retiring on 31 November 1886.

In spite of these efforts, according to the Royal Commission of 1869, 'the best labourers, the most active and intelligent lads in the villages, were leaving their native places for the towns, railways and large works, where labour commands a higher price than it does on the farm' and Kirby le Soken was no exception: Robert Burch, a carpenter, had become an engine driver by 1861. The sole parish charity founded by Doctor Avery on the 4th August 1719 had lapsed since 1812, so that the amount of capital had increased. In December 1847, the first distribution was made to the ten who were poor but not receiving parish relief. Care of the sick at the Essex and Colchester hospital was strictly limited leaving the major responsibility to the workhouses: a patient was treated only if nominated by a subscriber (including William Burgess), non-infectious, curable, sane, over seven years old, possessing a change of linen and orderly in behaviour. Robert Large Baker, son of Samuel, trained at Saint Bartholomew's hospital, was sole house surgeon from September 1841 until June 1844 assisted by a fifteen year old apprentice (1841) and a nursing staff of a matron, and five elderly nurses who lacked the training inaugurated by Florence Nightingale in the second half of the century.

After the dissolution of the monasteries in 1536 and 1539, care of the poor became the responsibility of the individual parish for which the overseers, elected by the vestry meeting and controlled by the magistrates, were responsible. In 1784, Gilbert's Act stated that the able bodied were no longer to be accommodated in workhouses, but provided with work at the public expense. In 1795, the justices of Speenhamland, Berkshire, used a system which became widely copied, of increasing relief to a minimum amount dependent on the price of wheat and supplement the wages of agricultural labourers. In an appreciative letter to the Home Secretary, dated 23 February 1837, The Tendring Board of Guardians wrote:—

> "That prior to the formation of this Union the single and married, the able bodied, the idle, disorderly and the dissolute Characters as well as the careful industrious labourer, were (as regarded the administration of relief) in many of the parishes of the Union, indiscriminately mixed up together, and each equally received a card allowance on a Scale according to the number of his family and the price of flour, from the parish Funds, making up a certain rate of wages whether employed or not, thus making the bad Character more careless as to obtaining an employment and leaving no stimulus for, but discouraging instead of encouraging the careful and industrious Labourer, by placing him on an equal footing only with the disorderly and idle."

Although this system was used in the Tendring Hundred, whether it was followed by Kirby le Soken, it is impossible to determine through lack of evidence.

In the summer of 1834 the Poor Law Amendment Act was passed by the newly enfranchised parliament. By this, parishes were grouped into Unions, each with a single workhouse, to provide for what Edwin Chadwick, Secretary to the three Poor Law Commissioners at Somerset House, regarded as 'the undeserving poor'. No longer were paupers to be given financial assistance except for sickness and old age. At local level, the Unions were administered by a board of Guardians elected by the ratepayers in each parish. The Board of Guardians of the Tendring Union (in 1839 including Harwich and Dovercourt) held its first meeting at the Maids Head Inn at Thorpe le Soken on the 18th November 1835 for instructions and explanations from Assistant Commissioner Alfred Power and in their first year, reduced expenditure on poor rate from £17,845 to £10,672. Guardians included ex officio the justices of the peace including: John Martin Leake Esq., of Thorpe Hall elected chairman, with Mr. Robert Canham Salmon, guardian of Beaumont as vice chairman, and Mr. Thomas Nunn J.P., treasurer on a surety of £1,500; a local solicitor was employed as clerk to the Board. Kirby le Soken was represented by Samuel Baker in these early years, and Frinton by Richard Stone of Frinton Hall.

The task before them was formidable: instead of a number of small parish workhouses, one was to be built to cater for the whole area, but until this was completed, the workhouse inmates needed accommodation. So the Union was divided into four districts: Thorpe (including Kirby and Walton), Maningtree, Saint Osyth (including Great Clacton) and Ardleigh, with a salaried relieving officer living in each district to deal with outdoor relief and reporting with his accounts at the weekly meeting on Wednesday at 10 o'clock in the forenoon. This first meeting appointed a committee of five to investigate the resources of the workhouses within the Union. Overseers continued to be responsible within the parish but a salaried assistant overseer collected and transferred the poor rate.

By the end of 1835, the Tendring Guardians had dealt with the most urgent essentials. The timetable for changes in parish relief was drawn up: money payments in the shops on behalf of paupers were to be discontinued as from 1st January 1836 'when the Poor Law becomes fully into operation in this Union', to be replaced by outdoor relief, half in money and half in bread, to the sick and infirm only. The committee recommended the extension of four workhouses: Mistley for the aged and infirm, with husbands and wives together; Thorpe for the able bodied males, and Saint Osyth for the able bodied females; under sixteen year olds went to Great Bromley, where the sexes were kept separate. Lists of paupers were revised in their presence, and those in the four Union houses chosen were given a month to quit or be dispossessed. Warrants were issued for the collection of the new poor rate, assessed on the needs of the Union as a whole, which in Kirby was £95. 15. of the total £2,230. 12. 6 half yearly. A married couple was appointed master and mistress for each workhouse at a salary of £50 a year, and at Thorpe, James Holby, already commended by the magistrates for his sense of duty during the Tendring riots, became its first master.

For the children at Great Bromley, a school master and mistress were appointed.

The Thorpe Guardians had their problems in purchasing equipment: the fifty 2 feet 6 inches iron beds at eighteen shillings each, bought from a Great Clacton blacksmith, were made with iron hoop bottoms which damaged the bedding and had to be replaced by sacking bottoms. The hessian mattress covers were filled monthly with straw at 6 pence a bed, the supplier having the use of the old filling. Blankets and counterpanes were bought, but it was three months before sheeting was ordered for sheets to be 'occasionally washed' and tableware consisted of tin quart basins and iron spoons. Diet Sheet Number 1, supplied by the Poor Law Commissioners, set out the ration for each meal: breakfast consisted of bread and gruel; dinner of meat and potatoes three times a week, soup three times and suet or rice pudding on Friday; supper of bread with cheese three days and broth, four. Old people over sixty were allowed 1 ounce of tea, 7 ounces of butter and 8 ounces of sugar per week 'in lieu of gruel for breakfast, if it seemed expedient to make the change'. Until 1856 when a special children's diet sheet was issued, children under nine were treated with discretion, and over nine allowed the same quantities as women. Sick people were fed as directed by the medical officer. The limited diet of able bodied labourers brought a request from the Tendring Guardians in March 1836 that the diet should be increased by an additional ½ pound of potatoes twice, and four ounces of bread, three times a week. Rules about workhouse clothing were uncompromising. On admission to the workhouse:—

> 'Paupers should be stript of all their clothing (with the exception of Shirts, Shifts and Stockings) and that in lieu of their own dress the Workhouse dress should be substituted, and that on every occasion when they leave the Workhouses, they should leave the Workhouse dress and resume their own clothing.'

The Guardians bought for men and boys: shoes, brown fustian suits, leather caps, shirts, shoes and worsted stockings, but no pants or vests; women and girls: shoes and blue worsted stockings, olive calico for petticoats and gowns, unbleached calico for shifts, pairs of stays. Stockings alone were made of wool.

Single men were not allowed out and the greatest problem for

Thorpe workhouse was to provide work for the able bodied men. A new hand mill was installed and the Guardians began in February 1836 by paying paupers six shillings a week for labour, with a deduction of six pence for lodging and diet — the money to be collected when the man left the Union house. Members of the public were charged three pence a bushel for grinding their wheat and barley. So successful was this work that within a fortnight, the Guardians decided to install an additional crank to the mill 'for the greater facility of employing an additional number of men' and employed an engineer at £3 a week, part of whose work was to organise a system of ventilation in the mill shed. But this payment was contrary to regulations and the Poor Law Commissioners ordered it to stop; an early lesson in government intervention.

Medical officers were appointed to deal with the sick, childbirth, surgical operations and to certify lunatics, who in these early years were maintained at Hoxton or Peckham asylums at Tendring's expense. A truck was bought to convey the dead pauper (usually from Mistley) to his own parish, a supply of coffins arranged and burial fees for paupers were laid down: clergy two shillings, clerk two shillings and two shillings for bearers. Some clergy objected. The Rev. Frank Storky was reprimanded for refusing to bury two children unless paid eight shillings for each. Two months later, the Guardians were even more annoyed and summoned the Rev. William Burgess's parish clerk to explain why two persons who died at Thorpe were buried in one grave. Perhaps Samuel Baker felt some satisfaction in proposing that:—

'It was ordered that one of the paupers so buried should be disinterred, and decently buried in another grave.

The vicar wrote twice in protest, only to be informed that there was no reason to pay him more than the fees in other parishes. The medical officers, together with the masters of the workhouses concerned, supervised the transfer of paupers of adult males and females to Mistley when aged or infirm and the sixteen year olds from Great Bromley to either Thorpe or Saint Osyth.

The legal importance of the date of birth, apart from the need of the workhouses, increased as Factory Acts to protect children became law and Union boundaries and districts were used for the Registration of Births, Marriages and Deaths as from 1st June 1837. Like the medical officers, the registrars (usually solicitors) were paid for their services, and their returns forwarded to the registrar-general at Somerset House. The 1836 Tithe Commutation Act gave similar responsibility to the Tendring Union in arranging for the detailed mapping of its parishes including fields names and types, produce, owner and tenant before the landowners came to an agreement with their tenants about the yearly payment to the owner of the great or vicarial tithe. Kirby le Soken was mapped by Messrs Ruffle and Joy.

Samuel Baker was one of the committee of three who regularly inspected Thorpe workhouse: the inmates repaired the clothing of the boys at Great Bromley; the master and mistress asked for a separate privy and a drain made to the adjoining ditch for the workhouse privy. Inspection was taken seriously and in April 1837 the Guardians dismissed the master of Great Bromley workhouse after an enquiry at which he was accused of letting children out for hire and taking their earnings; substituting red herring for meat and charging for meat; supplying his own family with provisions from store; selling coal from stock; allowing the schoolmistress to sell cakes to the children; sometimes sleeping away from the workhouse. Regular 'payment via the assistant overseer of the parish' was made to the Guardians for a bastard, brought up in the workhouse whenever the father accepted paternity as for Mary Powell, child of Sarah by Thomas Bundock. Clothes were provided for paupers going into service: Sarah Woods was given one pair of shoes, two pairs of stockings, two shifts, one underpetticoat, one skirt, one gown and one mantle apron when she went to work for Peter Bromley of Great Bentley. By the 1850s, servant girls earning the small wage of nine pence or a shilling a week and their keep, once more were forced to seek help. No abled bodied man belonging to an illegal club (trade union) operating among the farm labourers would be given relief 'now or in the future' and to make this clear, 500 copies of an address signed 'Your friend' was circulated by relieving officers among men in their districts.

From 5th October 1836 until completed, the building of the Tendring Union Workhouse became of prior importance. The design of Mr. Gilbert Scott of Carlton Chambers, London (early in his distinguished career) was accepted to house 400 inmates and costing £5,200 but unwisely reduced in size to 350 to economise. Choice of site between Tendring, Little Bentley and Weeley proved more difficult. Finally, the lord of the manor of New Hall, Tendring, sold an area on Tendring Heath to the Guardians for £400, and the building contract for £4,647 was again won by Joseph Salmon of Beaumont. First, engineers were employed to cut a drain, going through only one field, for sewage to empty into a covered tank and to sink a well containing 15 feet of standing water for transfer through iron pipes. A proportion of the cost was raised by the sale of the already empty parish workhouses, which by 1st January 1840 had raised £4,047. 14. The workhouse of Kirby le Soken was sold for £249. 19 together with three cottages near Kirby Brook but the sale of Townfield and Townfield Cottages on Kirby Lower Street was disallowed as being a charitable trust belonging to the parish. Gilbert Scott completed his designs and stabling for thirty horses and a gravelled approach to the main entrance. At the end of 1838, the Poor Law Commissioners provided a loan of £11,500 for building, which already had to include an extension above the stables to help house the inmates due to arrive during the week ending Friday, 14th of June 1839.

After the flurry caused by an anonymous letter stating that the newly appointed master and mistress were Roman Catholics, the inmates of the four temporary workhouses, carrying bedding and provisions for the day, arrived on successive days, beginning with the men of Thorpe followed by the women of Saint Osyth; on Thursday, the sick and aged from Mistley and finally, the children from Great Bromley. Wednesday was set aside for the arrival of all the inmates from Harwich workhouse. In the following week, the newly furnished and carpeted board room was used by the Guardians for the first time and kept for their sole use. In addition to a medical officer, chaplain, clerk to the Guardians, three relieving officers (Harwich, Ardleigh and Thorpe) instead of four officials were appointed in the following order:—

Porter — £20 per annum and board.
Master and Mistress — £100 per annum and board.
Schoolmistress — £20 per annum and rations.
Schoolmaster — £25 per annum and rations.
Ostler and Messenger — £12 per annum with rations.
Laundress (wife of the porter) — rations only.
Nurse for the infirmary — £10 per annum with board and lodging.

The early 1840s brought great distress, which possibly the Guardians recognised by allowing paupers 'to see their friends in this House' between nine and four on Thursdays only. From October 1840 a room was hired once a week at Kirby post office of Mr. John Daniels where at 11 a.m. on Tuesday, the area medical officer, Doctor Osmond, attended to vaccinate the poor of Kirby and Frinton and to inspect those who were sick or claiming outdoor relief. Many suffered from what was described as 'debility': Mrs Scowen, who was given outdoor relief from 17th December 1845, died at Kirby of phthysis (tuberculosis of the lungs) in the following year. At the same place, the relieving officer attended on the same day to distribute outdoor relief in terms of small sums of money and quartern loaves of bread and in 1842, the estimated poor rate of Kirby le Soken with 921 inhabitants was £352 for the financial year. The Tendring Union House became increasingly overcrowded creating problems with sanitation. In 1841 the workhouse began to brew beer for the staff and to bake its own bread under a baker's supervision. Boys were taught shoemaking, but the Guardians found it increasingly difficult to keep a schoolmistress. In January 1848 a work plan was defined: able-bodied poor must work for not more than four hours 'after breakfast on the morning after admission; the weaker to pick oakum (tease the fibres of old ropes) and no one given tasks unsuitable for age or strength. Women were divided up and bad characters separated: the aged given a day room, pregnant women put into the lying-in ward and two wards set aside for vagrants (with male and female separated), each with a workshop and access to the water closet. To share the cost of a shifting population which failed to qualify as parish residents for relief, the Guardians set up a common fund to which all parishes contributed.

In November 1848, the spread of cholera across Europe into England resulted in an act setting up the General Board of Health operating at local level through the Poor Law Unions. After finding an inspector of nuisances useless, Tendring Union appointed small committees to include two medical officers. By July 1849, with cholera in Harwich, the first isolation hospital was set up in a granary on the quay at Mistley. Harwich churchyard was so overcrowded that arrangements were made to bury the dead at Dovercourt. Owners of 'foul and offensive privies' were prosecuted, but the Guardians' efforts to organise a regular flushing of drains by the Harwich inhabitants was thwarted by the mayor. With increasing Poor Law expenditure, the decline of farming and the fall of prices, the Guardians reduced the wages of all their officers. When the Commissioners objected, they replied by letter:

> 'This Country in the Agricultural Districts is being brought to the same dilemma as now threatens our sister Kingdom and shortly to Irelandise England.' (A reference to the misery of the Irish Potato Famine.)

So the Commissioners compromised by agreeing to reduced fees for new appointments. By 1850, the Guardians were organising a lunatic rate to build the asylum at Warley, county rate and police rate and preparing to cover the cost of the 1851 census as they had done in 1841. In 1852 at the workhouse the well and its pump needed new machinery, pipes in the laundry were broken and battered and the Commissioners' inspector described the water closets thus:

> 'I cannot find one fit to use not having a supply of water to keep them clean the way now adopted is to wash them through with a pail. Each one should have a separate cistern.'

Not only labourers were affected by the farming recession. On 19th May 1852 on the surety of two Suffolk friends, James Coates employing two men to farm 89 acres at Blue House Farm, Kirby and a former Guardian, was elected relieving officer of Thorpe district at £85 per annum, after being assistant overseer of Kirby for a short period. He was reminded that he must keep a horse and cart for Union purposes and display a weekly list of persons receiving poor relief in the parish on each church door. Mr. Coates obtained special permission to reside just over the Thorpe border in Weeley at Brick House which still stands today. In company with parish guardians, medical officers, other relieving officers, clergymen, churchwardens, overseers and surveyors, he distributed Health Board regulations listing diseases caused by nuisances: cholera, diarrhoea, typhus or any frequent epidemic or endemic disease. In his first few years of office, John Coates took out two summons on behalf of the Guardians: Alfred Baker of Saville Street, Walton (son of Samuel Baker) complained of a nuisance certified by two medical officers to be in a 'filthy and unwholesome condition injurious to the health'; and Crooks Barton (son of the late Benjamin Barton of Kirby), assistant overseer of Walton, absconded with £70. 13. 8. of the poor rate, making his two sureties liable. It is possible that some members of James Coates' family were innocent victims of his profession; his daughter Fanny died of cerebral effusion in 1861, in January 1862 his eldest son of ulceration of the larynx and at the end of March, his wife, with bowel stoppage followed by his eldest daughter of fever on 31st March. On 2nd April, the 72 year old James Coates resigned his post as relieving officer and retired to Ipswich where he died in June, two months after the Reverend William Burgess, vicar of the Sokens.

The last years of the Tendring Union still under the chairmanship of J. M. Leake, J.P., were dogged by problems of overcrowding in the union house, and typhus fever and poverty in the parishes. The presentation to him of the silver salver and silver inkstand by the Guardians on his retirement at the beginning of 1862, marks the end of the era of paternalism. The Board of Guardians of the Tendring Hundred formed a transitional stage between common responsibility centred on the Parish Church and the secular approach towards centralisation.

KIRBY-LE-SOKEN (POPULATION 875) 17th APRIL 1861

I. POOR RELIEF ABSTRACT OF ACCOUNTS FOR HALF YEAR TO 17.4.1861

In Maintenance	Outdoor Relief	Lunatic Asylum	Extra Medical Fees
£16. 13. 11¾	£111. 2. 4½	£2	£1
Vaccination	Registration Fees	Common Fund	Coffin
£2. 17. 6	£1. 10	£63. 16. 5	12. 6

Final Total (Approx. in modern currency):—£199.60.

II. RATES COLLECTED THROUGH THE TENDRING UNION FROM KIRBY-LE-SOKEN

County	Police Rate	Lunatic Asylum	Total
£5. 6. 7	£5. 6. 7	£10. 13. 2	£21. 6. 4

Final Total Paid by Kirby-le-Soken to and through the Tendring Union (Approximate modern currency):—£220.90.

CHAPTER FIVE

The Reverend William Langston Coxhead

As he became older and in great demand as a visiting preacher, the Reverend William Burgess found it necessary to maintain curates in each of the three Sokens. On the 13th December 1841, the prosperous Reverend Warwell Fenn died after being curate of Kirby-le-Soken for seventeen years, with a stipend of £80 per annum, service fees (baptism, marriage and burial) and occupation of the newly built vicarage. To replace him, the Reverend William Coxhead M.A. arrived with his half-caste wife and baby daughter in May 1842 and was licensed as curate of the parish of Kirby-le-Soken on 10th June 1842 with a salary of £100 per annum and service fees to live in the vicarage.

William Langston Coxhead, born in Middlesex on 6th February, 1813 was the only son of Benjamin Lyon Coxhead, grocer, of 39, Cannon Street in the City of London and of Amelia née Langston, who died within a month of his birth; not until he was nine did his father marry Selina Cooper. Of the second family, two of the three girls lived well into the next century and maintained a close relationship with their half brother's adult daughters. William was about twelve when he joined the Homerton School for Young Gentlemen opened by the Reverend Thomas Burnet, D.D. at Sutton House in 1825, probably on the recommendation of Mr Lewis Berger, colour manufacturer of Well Court, just round the corner from the grocer. This 'first class Gentleman's Boarding School' based on the teaching of the Church of England and where the cane was used as at Eton, Harrow and Rugby, quickly gained a great reputation for scholarship, thanks to its headmaster who, in 1836 became Fellow of the Royal Society. Doctor Burnet's application was supported by ten leading scholars in zoology, natural history, medicine, astronomy, mathematics, social and sanitary reform besides Bible study, who also showed a practical involvement in dentistry and care of the destitute. William proved

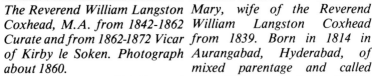

The Reverend William Langston Coxhead, M.A. from 1842-1862 Curate and from 1862-1872 Vicar of Kirby le Soken. Photograph about 1860.

Courtesy of M. Everard

Mary, wife of the Reverend William Langston Coxhead from 1839. Born in 1814 in Aurangabad, Hyderabad, of mixed parentage and called Mary Wilson, she died in 1861 in Kirby le Soken, where she is buried at the side of her husband in the churchyard. Photograph about 1860.

Courtesy of M. Everard

an able pupil and at the age of eighteen was admitted as a pensioner to Trinity College on 2nd July, 1832 at a time of great religious ferment in which the college played a leading part. After matriculating in October 1832, he graduated in 1836 and was registered as a Master of Arts in 1839 by which time he was ordained.

During the long summer vacations, sometime between 1833 and 1835, he visited Oaklands, a large mansion in Okehampton, Devonshire, probably to tutor the second son, Bourchier Wrey Savile, who was destined for Cambridge university and the church. This arrangement completely changed William Coxhead's life. Albany Savile, Oxford graduate, barrister at law and member of Parliament for Okehampton from 1807 until 1820, had built Oaklands which was completed by 24th September, 1821 to form the centre of a comparatively small estate. But on 26th January, 1831 Albany Savile died leaving his widow Eleanora Elizabeth (the daughter of Sir Bourchier Wrey, Baronet) with a young family. To educate her daughters and the small boys, the widow employed the young Mary Wilson as governess. There at Oaklands, the Cambridge undergraduate fell in love with the children's governess. So, instead of seeking a curacy near to London and marrying according to the wishes of his family, William Coxhead was ordained deacon at Bristol by letters dimissory from Exeter on 5th June, 1836, became curate at Holy Trinity church, Ilfracombe on 1st October, 1836 and was ordained as priest in the following year. The executors of Albany Savile were responsible for the patronage of the advowsons of Okehampton and King's Nympton to be presented to his sons in order of seniority, except for the eldest. If the living was vacant, presentation was to be made to a parson "entering in a Bond to resign the said Church or Living in favour of sons successively to be presented." The situation was cleverly adjusted: in 1838, the Reverend William Coxhead became curate of Okehampton, and lived with the Reverend James R. Whyte and his family at the very large grey stone rectory, probably spending much of his time teaching the boys of the Savile family. At the parish church on the 15th of October, 1839, the curate William Coxhead married the twenty five year old governess Mary Wilson with Eleanora Elizabeth Savile and James Whyte's eldest daughter, Mary Elizabeth, as witnesses. Because the second son was ordained in 1840 and already serving as curate at Halesowen, the Reverend James Whyte moved to the vacant living of King's Nympton in 1840, leaving William Coxhead as rector for nearly a year at Okehampton until the Reverend Bourchier Savile was finally inducted in 1841.

Away from the benevolent patronage of Eleanora Savile, the

Oakhampton, Devonshire. 1831 Lithograph of Oaklands, Oakhampton where Mary Wilson was employed as Governess to the children of the Savile family, until her marriage to the Reverend William Coxhead, October 15, 1839. The building still stands.

Exeter Record Office

young couple probably found life difficult because Mary Coxhead was Eurasian, born on 1st September, 1814 at Aurangabad in Hyderabad, the eldest daughter of a native woman and an Englishman. Because Mary's father was to make an important marriage in India, before the marriage contract was signed in 1817 or early in 1818, he sent his two small children to England in the charge of their ayah to be educated and brought up in Devonshire. Financial arrangements were made for their upkeep including the purchase of an annuity, and the importance of secrecy was emphasised. On the long voyage the little boy died and was buried at sea, but Mary was met, according to previous arrangement, by a man of law, Mr. Holroyd, who took her to a school, probably in Exeter, where she was brought up as Mary Wilson. According to descendants, her memories of India were few, but included the pictures of a crying woman standing on the quay, waving to the children as the ship left the harbour. The name 'Holroyd' given to the eldest child of William and Mary was explained away as a compliment to the lawyer, who treated Mary very kindly when she arrived in England.

It is difficult to decide how much Mary ever knew about her background: in the 1851 census her place of birth is given as "East Indies", but in 1861 as "Avingabad, India" (correctly spelled Aurangabad); from the only existing photograph, her mixed blood is apparent; on her marriage certificate, her father is unnamed. The large crayon drawings, including 'L'Enfant Jesus' in black and white and the coloured 'Madonna and Child' owned by her descendants show the careful but limited technical skill required as a governess teaching in the wealthy Savile household for about eight years where she was obviously regarded as intelligent and capable.

So far, the story of Mary Wilson is based on documentary evidence and family history, but it is possible to identify her father by the association of names and events. The lawyer, George Sowley Holroyd was born in York on 31st October, 1758, educated at Harrow, but university was impossible because of his father's debts. To qualify as a solicitor, he was articled in April, 1774 to Mr. Borthwick, a London attorney and in 1777 transferred to the chambers of Sir Alan Chambre in Gray's Inn. In 1779, he became a special pleader, and with Sir Samuel Romilly (who was to be one of the leaders in reform of prisons and the criminal code) Christian and Baynes, founded a legal debating society. After being called to the Bar on 26th June, 1787, he worked on the northern circuit and at Westminster, but refused to become a king's counsel. In 1811, he was distinguished in the case of Burdett v. Abbott in which he acted for the plaintiff who was well known for his liberal views. After being sent as commissioner to Guernsey in 1815 to study their grievances, George Holroyd was made a judge of King's Bench on 14th February, 1816 where he earned a great reputation for learning and courtesy, and was knighted three months later. His eldest son, George Chaplin Holroyd, born in London on 9th September, 1790, went to Harrow and spent a few months from 1808 to 1809 at Trinity College, Cambridge. England was fighting Napoleon, not only in Europe but also in the East Indies and in 1809, George Holroyd joined the army of the East India Company. On the voyage to India in 1810 on the "Astell", he distinguished himself in action against the French and was wounded. From 1811 until 1815 he served as an ensign in the Bengal army stationed in Hyderabad (Mary Wilson was born in September, 1814) and in

1815 became lieutenant in the 29th Bengal Native Infantry.

By 1818, British India was ruled by the East India Company's servants, and other areas indirectly through Indian princes controlled by treaties, troops and resident advisers. On 25th November, 1817, Lieutenant George Chaplin Holroyd was named as commander of the escort of Henry Russell, British Resident at the court of the Nizam of Hyderabad. In the Autumn of 1817, Lieutenant Charles Holroyd, R.N., arrived in Madras to witness on 2nd April, 1818, the important political and social marriage of his brother, George Chaplin Holroyd with Virginie, daughter of General Mottet, the French Governor of Pondicherry and the ceremony performed by the British Resident. On 18th July, 1828 George Chaplin Holroyd resigned with the rank of captain, probably because ill health forced his father to retire in the November; Sir George died three years later at Hare Hatch in Berkshire. At about the time Mary Wilson was completing her education, Captain Holroyd took his wife and family to live at 18 Southernay, Exeter where he administered the branch Bank of England at his home and finally became a partner in the Devonshire County Bank, later merged into the National Provincial Bank of England. The Holroyd link with India continued with three sons serving in the Bengal army and his eldest daughter marrying a lieutenant-colonel in 1850. Three years after the death of his wife, called in England Mary Virginie, on 14th August, 1848 George married Frances (Fanny) Harrington and died on 25th November, 1871 aged eighty two, leaving a fortune of £40,000.

In his introduction to "Sermons Doctrinal and Practical" by Reverend William Burgess, B.D., "printed with a view of forming a memorial of the late esteemed author" and published at Colchester in 1863, the William Coxhead pays tribute to the late vicar's "friendship for twenty years" which began with his appointment as curate in 1842 at what must have been a time of great difficulty for the young couple. From September, 1841 until April, 1842 William assisted at St. Pancras parish church and his eldest child, Mary Holroyd, was born on the 4th of December, 1841 at Pratt Street, Camden Town where they became close family friends of Mark Fothergill, gentleman of Havistock Hill and of his future son in law, Septimus Pattison. But a permanent living was essential and, apart from recommendation by the Bishop of London, the nature of the link between the Rev. William Burgess and the young clergyman is open to conjecture. A possible intermediary was the Reverend John Whiting born at Cawnpore, North India in 1828, the son of the chaplain to the Reverend Wilson, D.D. Lord Bishop of Calcutta from 1832 to 1858; the Rev. Whiting became an esteemed friend of the Rev. and Mrs. Burgess and was named as one of the four trustees to administer the patronage of the Sokens in the will of Mrs. Burgess made in 1862. On the other hand, George Chaplin Holroyd's brother, James J. Holroyd, was rector of Abberton, Essex from 1838 to 1876 but lived in Colchester where the preaching of William Burgess on behalf of the British and Foreign Bible Society made them acquainted. The personal diaries of Doctor Burnet which might have supplied important information on this matter, remain untraced.

The young curate and his wife settled happily in Kirby le Soken, although money became short with the family enlarged by the birth of a child every eighteen months to two years, until the youngest, George Lyon was born in September, 1857, making nine children in all. So, whereas in 1851, two adult women helped at the Vicarage, in 1861 one fourteen year old maid servant was employed. With frequent pregnancies, a large family and decreasing domestic help, Mary Coxhead took little part in parish affairs except for acting as treasurer of the Kirby branch of the Colchester and East Essex Bible Society with her husband as secretary, a duty required by William Burgess of all his clergy and their wives, including Mrs. Burgess.

On 4th June, 1861, Mary Coxhead died aged forty six and was buried in Kirby Churchyard; less than a year later, on the death of William Burgess, William Coxhead became vicar of Kirby le Soken after serving as its curate for twenty years.

CHAPTER SIX

Education

*'The intellectual instruction of the children is
lamentably below the requirements of the age.'
(Headmaster, Doctor Jacob, addressing the Court
and scholars of Christ's Hospital.)*

On January 13, 1873, the school for 135 children built by The
National Society for Promoting the Education of the Poor in the
Principles of the Established Church was opened in Kirby le Soken
(where the church hall stands today) with a certificated headmaster,
an untrained woman assistant and one pupil teacher, two years
after elementary education in the three R's to the age of thirteen
became compulsory and more than a decade after the death of the
Reverend William Burgess. Until that time, many of 'the poor'
learned to read and write either at Sunday school or while inside the
Union workhouse.

The school room built in 1828 by William Burgess at his own
expense in the Kirby le Soken churchyard was extended five years
later to take 150. The room was 'divided in the Centre by a shifting
partition, that the sexes may be taught separately' in two large
classes, and was open for scholars every Sunday at 9 a.m. and 2
p.m. The school, supervised by the minister, was maintained by
voluntary contribution (about ten pounds a year) and scholars were
not asked to contribute. In 1839, about 28 of the 39 males on the
register attended and 65 of the 81 females; but by 1841 numbers on
the books had fallen to 30 males and 68 females. However,
education became important to the Church of England, which had
set up the National Society to carry out its programme. In 1841,
Saint Mark's, its first college of education was founded at Chelsea;
nearer home, colleges of education for training schoolmistresses
were established in 1851 at Hockerill and Bishop's Stortford. In
this atmosphere, Kirby Day School opened in the existing building

during the 1850s, where the children were taught religion, reading, writing and arithmetic by Mrs. Mary Lott (wife of the village grocer) and the curate. In 1860, Kirby school, where pupils paid a penny a week, had an average attendance of 65 out of the 79 on the register, and was maintained largely by voluntary contributions. The growth of literacy is obvious both in the marriage register and in tradesmen's bills.

Better education was found in the Tendring union workhouse where the schooling of children to the age of fourteen was compulsory and regular under the direction of a full-time schoolmaster and schoolmistress. By the very nature of the environment, a combination of practical subjects and elementary instruction was inevitable and worked well: girls learned cookery, laundry and needlework; boys worked in the gardens and at shoemaking under the direction of a professional shoemaker. Teaching was subject to inspection by representatives of the Poor Law Commissioners who maintained a secular outlook on education, leaving the workhouse chaplain appointed from local parish clergy to deal with spiritual matters. The improved reading standards were reflected by the Guardians' purchase from the Society for the Promotion of Christian Knowledge of books for 'Boys and Girls in the Workhouse during their recreation hours'. (See Appendix III) Although the reading matter was instructive, either supplying information such as *The Conquest of Peru,* or providing a moral lesson as in *Unselfishness or the Miner's Daughter,* the formation of a library of 31 titles was a great step forward.

Apart from Miss Elizabeth Savage who, in the early part of the period, owned a small boarding school on the Lower Street, no education facilities existed in Kirby le Soken for the sons and daughters of farmers, and most were sent away to small private schools in the area. In 1830, at both Hill House Academy in Manningtree and Thorpe Academy, boys used copy books for arithmetic, grammar and catechism, as well as slates. But the Kirby farmers tended to send their sons in a group to larger schools kept by reputable masters. The school favoured in the 1830s until 1841 was that of Mr. William Parris's school in Sir Isaac's Walk, Colchester, which in 1841 employed two resident teachers and four servants. This school, considered suitable by William Burgess, by

71

1835 received Alfred and William, sons of the missionary, the Reverend Henry Baker, when he was on leave from India, and the seven year old Samuel was sent in January 1841. At the same school in 1841 was the youngest son of Mr. Samuel Baker of Birch Hall, with sons of powerful farmers of Walton, Beaumont and Great Oakley. But two events changed the situation: the Reverend William Burgess was unable to continue responsibility for Henry Baker's children and Fanny Salmon of Great Oakley married Mr. Catling of Copford, Essex, near a new boy's boarding school, established at Kelvedon, and, as a young widow, in 1839 married its headmaster.

By 1841, Henry Baker's eldest son, Henry, was a student at the Church Missionary Society College at Highbury, Islington, which left the ageing Reverend and Mrs. Burgess with the task of dealing with the problems of two girls at school in the area and the three boys at Mr. Parris's school, a responsibility which included catering for their holidays. When new arrangements were made at Burgess's request, the boys were sent to the C.M.S. school, King William's College, Isle of Man, the elder girl returned to India and Mary Ann went to St. Mary's School for the Daughters of Clergy (now St. Mary's Hall) at Brighton. By 1844 the headmistress was anxious about her health and tactfully advised a return to a warmer climate, and Mary Ann left in 1845; in 1848 the two youngest girls, due to arrive in England, were refused places. Nevertheless, they sailed from Bombay, hoping that the younger would be accepted at Brighton and the elder placed for one year somewhere where she could learn drawing in which she had some proficiency. But with the increasing number of missionaries, in 1846 the C.M.S. had opened a school for their children in three houses in Milner Square, Islington, and there the Society sent the two girls, which angered their father, Henry Baker. However, he wrote to apologise to the Secretary, after receiving satisfactory details of the education of Susannah and Fanny. By the time the C.M.S. opened a newly-built home in Highbury Grove to receive and educate all the children of missionaries, Henry's youngest boy, then ten years' old, was due to arrive. On this occasion some sort of guidance was forwarded:

> 'Robert has never been from the care of his parents, his disposition is mild he is fond of reading interesting works, and of singing but is a stranger to the love of study. He has

had measles and whooping cough but neither ringworm
scarlet fever nor small pox. He has been vaccinated and the
complaint took very well.'

The complexity of the problem of educating the children of a
missionary overseas and occupying them during the school holidays
is illustrated by a letter dated 17th August, 1851 from Susannah at
Milner Square to her mother. After mentioning that she and sister
Fanny spent three weeks with Miss Savage in Colchester, she
continues:

'We stayed with Mrs. Burgess for ten days and I was alone at
Mr. Newells for three weeks. Mr. and Mrs. Burgess were very
poorly when we were there indeed he has been very ill.'

The Home helped to solve the problem, but the Rev. Henry
Baker Junior, when on leave in 1861, wrote a strongly worded letter
to the C.M.S. Secretary, protesting that too much money was being
spent on the care and education of missionary offspring.

For more than twenty years, Kelvedon became the educational
centre of the sons of Kirby farmers. By 1837, Mr. William
Wiseman had opened Kelvedon School, a 'Classical and
Commercial Academy for boys' in Church Street. With a resident
staff of two assistants including the twenty year old Mr. Richard
Read Willis and three female servants, the school catered for at
least forty boarders, among whom were the four sons of Richard
Stone of Frinton Hall. When the young widow, Fanny Catling
married Mr. Wiseman, the school expanded to at least a hundred
resident pupils. In 1851 Mr. Wiseman, M.C.P., described the
objects of the school as ensuring 'a thoroughly Scriptural and
Gentlemanly Education'; sound 'Classical and Mathematical
Education for pupils preparing for Universities, Military and Naval
Colleges or Learned Professions' to include chemistry, business
instruction with daily practice in modern continental languages;
strict but not rigorous discipline and industry stimulated by a
'judicious system of Reports, detailing amount of work and
position in class'. All pupils were treated as members of the same
household and provided with domestic comfort at 'the same table
as the Principal and his family'. Fees were inclusive of all items
except extras of a purely personal nature, and to avoid expense to
parents, pupils were loaned all necessary books, scientific readings,
maps and charts for a yearly charge of five shillings (25p) for each

language learned. The large buildings, which stand to-day, were described as 'commodious and spacious comprising well ventilated dormitories, a large and lofty school room, dining room, lavatory, laboratory and lecture room fitted with scientific apparatus'. Summer and Winter playgrounds were ample, 'the latter well drained and furnished with protection against the wet'.

Scale of Fees at Kelvedon School 1851

Pupils under 12	25 guineas per annum
over 12	30 guineas
Parlour boarders	40 guineas

Gentlemen preparing for universities 60 to 100 guineas according to accommodation required.

In his report dated 21st June, 1851, of the midsummer examination, Mr. Robert Lee of the College of Preceptors, reported that he examined 100 pupils in Greek and Latin classics, French and German, English history, grammar, geography, mathematics including mental arithmetic, algebra, Euclid elements, and one or two branches of natural philosophy (science). Higher grade certificates were awarded to four, including the Principal's sixteen year old stepson, William Catling; sixteen thirteen year olds obtained second class certificates; eight younger pupils received honourable mention after being examined mostly in English subjects.

Richard Read Willis, after gaining experience at Kelvedon School, set up his own Classical and Commercial Academy almost next door and included a Frenchman on the staff. So at Brunswick House in 1851, at half the fees charged by Mr. Wiseman, among the 48 boarders were Charles, the son of John Dennis Daniels and the two sons of the third marriage of the deceased Richard Stone of Willow Farm, Hector and Arthur. After leaving the boarding school of Miss Sarah Leabon at Thorpe (fees £12 a year), the nine year old Hector joined his brother, Arthur, where their joint school fees at Brunswick House for 1851 were £26 per annum. Both Kelvedon School and Brunswick House provided an educational background which did much to contribute to their later success as London businessmen.

But the curate, the Reverend W. L. Coxhead, M.A., with an income of less than £150 per annum, including service fees and his wife's small annuity, needed more than education for his four

Kelvedon (1981)—Church Street. Part of the Buildings of the School of Mr. William Wiseman (1840 to 1874) attended by the sons of Richard Stone of Frinton Hall.

boys. Like many poor clergy, he needed the help of schools recognised by the Charity Commissioners, which would provide food, clothing and pocket money for boys between eight and fifteen. In 1851, Saint John's Foundation was set up to provide choir boys from sons of poor clergy for the church of Saint Mark, in Saint John's Wood. They were boarded, educated and trained by the curate of St. Mark and the eldest son, William Routh Coxhead, was among its first pupils. In December 1852, the school separated from Saint Mark's and its pupils were transferred to Clapton House, Walthamstow. The committee that ran Saint John's School for half a century was dedicated to the task of seeking out the most deserving cases. In 1861, the association with private pupils of the headmaster was broken and the Committee appointed the Reverend E. C. Hawkins, M.A., to take charge of the new school at Leatherhead, where the third son, Edward Langston Coxhead was a pupil from 1861 to 1866; one of the first under the new regime which provided a grammar school education, together with games and athletic activities. Every Wednesday, each boy received threepence pocket money, and the tuck shop was kept busy.

The second son attended Christ's Hospital, founded by Edward VI for boys and girls needing assistance towards education and maintenance. By donating £500 towards the school's expenses, contributors were entitled to membership of the Court which selected the Council of Almoners that controlled the school which in 1858 totalled 1,302, housed in London and Hertford. Petition number 86 dated 6 March 1858, was presented by James Watts Russell, Esq., and Benjamin Walter Coxhead, aged eight, was 'Admitted, Court and Clothed' on April 20th. The petition of William Coxhead

> 'humbly sheweth that the Petitioner is a Clerk in Holy Orders, Curate whose income does not exceed £150 per annum with Wife and nine children altogether dependent on him,'

and certifies 'that the child is entirely at the disposal of the Governors until fifteen or when the Governors require'. The document was signed by the vicar of the Sokens, the churchwardens (John Dennis Daniels and Henry Baker) and three housekeepers (James Shum, William Orpen and John Hignell). Certificates supporting the petition were copies of Benjamin's baptism entry and of his parents' marriage. Boys and the few girls were sent to the school at Hertford where they remained until proficient at reading and writing; only then were they transferred to the great London School in the area of Newgate Street. Traditionally, apart from the music school which overlapped other departments, pupils were educated either in the writing school (joined by Benjamin Coxhead), which had a commercial bias, the grammar school or the mathematical school, founded by Charles II to provide a nautical education, and closely linked with Trinity House to keep instruction up-to-date. Senior boys were examined annually by representatives of Oxford and Cambridge universities and many remained at school until entering university. From 1853 to 1868, the upper grammar school headmaster, Doctor Jacob, worked hard to stimulate education, and 'his merits as a scholar and especially as a teacher' were beyond dispute. During his regime, less emphasis was placed on Greek, and French and German were introduced. The uniform provided was a long black woollen coat lined with bright yellow and buttoned to the waist by silvered metal buttons embossed with the profile of Edward VI, with a white linen cravat, black knee breeches, yellow stockings, black buckled shoes and, in winter, a long yellow shapeless smock under the coat.

By the time that the youngest son, George Lyon Coxhead, was ready for school, the situation had changed: the Reverend William Coxhead was Vicar of Kirby le Soken with a salary of £195 per annum and the number of dependents considerably reduced. However, the archdeacon's report of 1868 states that 'the poor worthy Vicar is in sad health' and was forced to employ a curate. So, at the age of thirteen, George was nominated by Colchester town council to be one of the twenty foundation scholars with free education at the Colchester Royal Grammar School (Charter 1584) in Lexden Road. When George entered the school in 1870, under new statutes drawn up by the Bishop of London and the Dean of Saint Paul's, the Rev. William Wright, M.A., D.C.L. was headmaster of a school of 53 boys including 17 boarders and had been busy re-organising the system of education, adding new subjects, including ancient and modern history, arithmetic and geometry to the study of classical Latin and Greek and insisting on the importance of games and physical recreation.

1851 Scale of Fees at the Elizabeth I
Royal Grammar School, Colchester
Upper School

Day Pupils—12 guineas per annum payable quarterly in advance
Boarders—Above 14—60 guineas
　　　　　　　Under 14—50 guineas
Books and Stationery extra
Lower School
Admission between 6 and 9; Terms 8 guineas per annum.

'The Class is grounded in Church Catechism, Scripture History, Reading, Writing, Spelling, Elements of Latin, French and Arithmetic, properties of Natural and Artificial Objects and Outlines of History and Geography.'

Another solution to the educational problems of middle-class boys was to send them to the household of a clergyman as a resident pupil. The C.M.S. sent Henry Baker Senior to the Rev. Thomas Rogers of Wakefield after he resigned from the headship of Wakefield Grammar School in 1814. An advertisement in the 1832 publication of Thomas Rogers' biography by his son, Charles, indicates the general acceptance of this method:

> 'The Reverend C. Rogers receives into his house young gentlemen to be instructed in the usual branches of Classical and Commercial Education. Terms £50 per annum because no extra charge except for washing and articles supplied—Sowerby Bridge, Halifax.

To ensure that Henry Baker Junior was given a satisfactory education, the Rev. William Burgess bought the advowson of St. Stephen's, Ipswich, where the Rev. Isaac Kitchin, installed as rector, taught Henry in his household for five years from the age of fourteen.

Girls' education suffered because of the indifference of most parents. At Christ's Hospital only 3% of the pupils were girls, yet Kirby Sunday school attracted three times as many girls as boys from the labouring classes. But there were exceptions: Richard Stone of Frinton Hall employed a governess, Elizabeth Laker, daughter of William Laker, originally a farmer in Little Bentley, who ran a very successful boarding school at Holbrook, Suffolk; from Frinton Hall, the youngest girl joined William Coxhead's lessons for his own daughters, particularly in mathematics.

A more important project was the establishment in 1832 by the Rev. Henry Venn Elliott of St. Mary's chapel, Rock Gardens, Brighton, of a school for the daughters of clergy to serve as a 'nursery for governesses for the higher and middle classes'. When the daughter of the missionary, Mary Ann Agatha Baker, entered St. Mary's Hall on 1st August, 1841 (entry number 165) the school had reached its full complement of 100 pupils, 16 governesses and 18 servants under the lady superintendent, Miss Tomkinson. The age of admission was between nine and fourteen, but subject to being able to read and spell with ease and versed in the first four rules of arithmetic'.

Each child pays £20 per annum for which she is taught the usual branches of English and French Education; the latter by two Parisian ladies, governesses of the institution. Music is an extra £3 per annum; Drawing £4; but the Trustees reserve to themselves in the case of each pupil, the decision whether, after due trial, there is prospect of success to justify the prosecution of these accomplishments.'

The only holiday in the year was between 1st June and 1st August, but pupils could be visited every day except Sunday by parents or guardians and taken out.

Mary Ann's clothing list makes interesting reading: 'Each child is to bring with her:—

A Bible and Prayer Book
A new umbrella
Workbag and sewing
  implements
Combs, brushes and gloves
6 day shifts
4 night shifts
3 night caps
2 flannel petticoats
3 white upper petticoats
Two pockets

8 pocket handkerchiefs
8 pairs of white cotton stockings
4 pairs of lamb's wool stockings
4 brown holland pinafores or
  aprons
2 short coloured dressing gowns
1 flannel dressing gown
2 pairs of shoes
1 pair of thick shoes or boots
A silver dessert spoon, tea
  spoon and fork, which will
  be returned.'

The Hall provided frocks, tippets (small capes of fur), cloaks, shawls and bonnets for its pupils.

But in 1845, she was forced to leave the school, because:

'The Trustees request that no child may be sent whose delicacy of health will demand extraordinary attention, or impede her studies . . . St. Mary's Hall, though offering in sea air, the size of its rooms and other arrangements, peculiar advantages for health, is not intended to recover sickly constitutions, but to train up its pupils in true religion and sound learning, in the hope that those whose abilities and circumstances permit will go forth as governesses, to educate others in the principles in which they have been educated themselves.'

During the Rev. William Burgess's lifetime, in spite of his efforts on behalf of individuals and of the labouring people of Kirby le Soken, the pattern of education was almost haphazard. But individual enterprise and the new approach of schools like St. John's Leatherhead, Christ's Hospital, Colchester Royal Grammar and St. Mary's Hall, Brighton, foreshadowed the turning point in 1870 by the first Act of Parliament which made elementary education compulsory for Kirby boys and girls with trained teachers in a society which was becoming increasingly industrialised.

APPENDIX III

BOOKS FOR CHILDREN IN THE TENDRING UNION WORKHOUSE—14th APRIL 1852

Ordered that the following books to be lent to the Boys and Girls in the Workhouse during their recreation hours and which the Society for Promoting Christian Knowledge had on the application of the Reverend Geo. Burmester agreed to supply at less than cost price to be obtained (viz).

	£.	s.	d.
Columbus Life & Discoveries		1.	11
Conquest of Peru			9
Curiosities & Wonders of the Vegetable Kingdom		1.	6
Labourers useful hints to — 2 parts		2.	3
Minerals & Metals—their natural History		1.	11
Conversations on the Parables			
(Lord Stanley Earl of Derby)		1.	3
Captain Cooks Life & Voyages		1.	11
Penny Sunday Reader the 3 first vols		6.	6
Insects their habitations			9
Bishop Stanley's Familiar History of Birds		3.	9
The Apricot Tree			½

	£.	s.	d.
Arthur Granville			3
Aunt Rachel & her Godson			3
Bear & Forbear			¾
The Broken Arm		1.	9
Charlie Burton			9
The Good Neighbour			6
The Instructor Vol. 1 to 5 only		7.	6
Little Dora Playfair			¾
Little Mountaineer			¾
Mary & Charlie			3
Old Adamson			1 ½
Pest of the Village			1 ½
The Railroad Labourer			1 ½
Thos. Kenmer or the events of a week			1 ½
Tomorrow			1 ½
The Emigrant Family			3
Twin Sisters			3
Unselfishness or the Miners Daughter			3
Widow Gray			¾
The widow & her son			1 ½
	1.15.7 ½		

81

CHAPTER SEVEN

I   *Music in the Church*

'*Everyone must feel and acknowledge the noble effect produced by a whole congregation rising and singing the praises of their Creator and Redeemer.*'

(Reverend Wm. Burgess — Preface to Hymns 7th Edition 1853).

The musical history of the parish church of Kirby le Soken begins to take shape at the dedication service on the afternoon of Wednesday, 16th October, 1833. At a time when music played little serious part in church services, supported by the violincello, the anthems sung 'by several Gentlemen who have offered their services' were unusually ambitious. Most of the items were composed by Kent whose anthems are described by a modern critic as 'smooth and even productions, generally pleasing but rarely rising above mediocrity', but in the 1830's his sacred music, especially the version of *Hear My Prayer*, was very popular. By being supplied with details of the anthems, members of the congregation became emotionally involved in the musical act of worship. (See Appendix)

This rebuilding of Kirby parish church coincided with a rebirth of religious purpose within the Church of England which found expression not only among scholars in the Oxford Movement, but in a more practical stimulus to reverence involving the congregation in the act of worship and in this, Trinity College, Cambridge played a leading part. Unlike today's congregations which sing psalms, hymns and responses, worshippers took little active part in the service. The parish clerk's main duty was to say the responses; in the west gallery, when there was no organ, an untrained choir and a medley group of musicians provided any music needed, usually of metrical psalms. But by the 1840's, parish churches became affected by the growing Church of England policy of regarding congregational singing as a necessary part of children's education as well as an act of worship. In 1833 the Society for the Promotion of Christian Knowledge, published John Turner's *Manual of Vocal Instruction* ('Chiefly with a view to Psalmody') and Sarah Ann Glover, a Norwich schoolteacher attracted so much attention by her successful system of teaching music that in 1835, she finally published her *Scheme to Render Psalmody Congregational* followed in 1845 by *The Manual of the Norwich Sol fa System.* Although these books were widely read and used, the singing classes at Exeter Hall attracted most publicity. Exeter Hall in London's Strand was opened in 1831 for meetings of religious and philanthropic bodies and provided the biggest concert hall in London until the Albert Hall was opened in 1871; the Reverend William Burgess owned Exeter Hall Share Certificates 183 and 184. There in 1841, under the auspices of Doctor James Kay, Secretary to the Committee of the Privy Council for Education and with its sanction, John Hullah held massed singing classes for at first schoolmasters, then schoolmistresses and by the end of the year, for the general public. Teachers completing the course were awarded a certificate of 'Competence to Teach Music from Hullah's Manual'. In this atmosphere the National Society for Promoting the Education of the Poor founded its first college for training men teachers, Saint Marks, Chelsea. There John Hullah was directed to establish a daily choral service sung in the chapel by students assisted by boys selected from the model school established in its grounds. The College under its principal, the Reverend D. Coleridge, vice-principal Thomas Helmore and the inspired John Hullah, was described in 1846 as 'the institution of modern times that has done much for the Choral Music of England'.

But in spite of the development of railways, most enthusiastic country parsons were unable to attend the centres of the choral revival. For them the amateur musician Doctor Robert Druitt of Curzon Street, Mayfair, who formed the Society for Promoting Church Music, provided the better solution. In its first issue of *The*

Parish Choir in February, 1846, the Society stated that 'something may be done and ought to be done, to improve the style of music and singing in our churches'. This eight-paged monthly publication gave practical advice for priests, choirs and organists, insisting that singing was 'a healthful and cheerful exercise' not only for children at school, but for adults in the congregation. The first editorial pointed out that 'Singing in church ought not to be left as a mere matter of accident . . . but that it ought to have all due arrangement and forethought'. Monthly, a music supplement was published beginning in the first number with a series of single chants adapted to the morning and evening psalms in the Prayer Book for every day of the month until in its six years of life, *The Parish Choir* had 'set forth and illustrated both the principles and details of the Church Services, as contained in *The Book of Common Prayer*' and had 'shown how they may best be celebrated both chorally and congregationally' and supplied at a cheap rate the music necessary to that end'. *The Parish Choir* insisted that the Anglican chants for the psalms and canticles which it had published were preferable to Gregorian chants which parishioners would find strange and difficult, and acted as an information and enquiry centre on parish church music. To assist church music, much had to be done to encourage changes in church furnishings which formed obstacles to congregational singing. In 1836, the undergraduates of Trinity College, Cambridge including William Coxhead, not only had insisted upon regular and devout daily worship by all members of the College, but in May, 1839 three of their number created 'The Cambridge Camden Society' with a monthly journal *The Ecclesiologist*. High pews and a three tiered pulpit, often in the centre of the chancel where it obscured the Communion Table, made unity of worship difficult, and the Camden Society quickly realised that the practice of using the west gallery for the choir with musicians or organ, limited their usefulness to both priest and congregation. So as part of the religious regeneration in parish churches, a new attitude towards church furnishings became an essential element of the musical scene.

Although Kirby le Soken with its much repaired 'servis' books was geographically remote from the choral revival, the activities of the Reverend William Burgess, who travelled widely to preach on behalf of the British and Foreign Bible Society, combined with a series of coincidences, kept the parish well aware of the exciting developments within the Church of England, even before the publication of *The Parish Choir.* In the preceding year Burgess bought for Thorpe the large second hand barrel organ (immediately fingered), the enthusiastic Reverend John Frere from Trinity College became curate of Hadleigh, Suffolk, the home of the wealthy Rand family: Susan was already the wife of Robert Mumford of Kirby Hall and in 1835, Richard Stone of Frinton Hall married her sister, Mary. In 1839, the association with John Frere was strengthened by his marriage to the daughter of the rector of Kelvedon where from 1839, sons of Kirby farmers were educated and attended the parish church. Finally, Frere became vicar of Cottenham a few miles from Cambridge in the native area of William Burgess's family, where already in nearby Over, another priest was building up a choir with the help of the village schoolmaster. Plainsong and the great religious music of the previous centuries were not for Cambridge villages, but from 1842, Frere fought a battle against the old custom of providing haphazard religious music. Choir and musicians walked out with their fifes, fiddles, clarionetes and a double bass. After some months, he then used Sarah Ann Glover's methods to train a choir of men, boys and girls with the help of the schoolmaster and accompanied by a violincello, until in 1847 the church acquired a fingered barrel organ (still in use today). This story was read with interest by readers of *The Parish Choir* in 1847. In this religious revival, like many other clergy, William Burgess published his book:

> *'Hymns for the Principal Festivals etc., with a selection of Psalms intended for the use of Churches in General, but more particularly for those of Thorpe, Kirby and Walton le Soken.'*
>
> (7th Edition 1853)

Kirby replaced its parish band and violincello by the purchase of a seraphine. A letter dated 13th May, 1838 was forwarded to Mr James Mason, their professional 'cellist:

> We, the undersigned, the Minister, Churchwardens, and principal Parishioners, in consideration of his past services, do hereby request James Collison Mason to accept the Violincello now in his possession, and belonging to the Parish, and to consider the same henceforth his own. We also

tender our thanks for his past Services in addition to the Sum of Three Pounds 2/- agreed to be paid to him out of the Church rate at the last Easter Meeting.

Warwell Fenn.	Minister.
J. Foaker	
Saml. Baker	Churchwardens.
Elizabeth Barnard	
John D. Daniels	
Rob Mumford	Principal
Richard Stone	Inhabitants.
Wm. Wilson	

The seraphine, regarded as a forerunner of the harmonium, was first sold in England in 1831 by John Green of Soho Square, with free lessons given on the premises. However, although the low price of forty guineas brought it within the income of such churches as Kirby as a substitute for an organ, its popularity was short-lived because of its 'harsh and rasping tone'. The instrument which stood on four slender legs, had a single manual of four octaves, no stops and two small foot pedals which operated the bellows inside; when closed it looked like an oblong table. From the date of the purchase in 1839, the churchwardens employed a professional musician from Colchester whose annual salary during the 1840's and'50s was between eight and nine pounds a year, but from the few records that exist, it is possible that in 1857 Kirby may have bought a small organ or harmonium. William Burgess's book measured 5½ inches by 3½ inches (about 113cm by 82 cm), the usual size of a hymn book today. Its 174 pages contained 101 hymns, 93 metrical psalms (several with alternative versions) 6 Gloria Patri and a single benediction provided the Soken with a book of worship, prior to the publication of *Hymns Ancient and Modern* in 1861. Both hymns and psalms were numbered in Roman figures, but fortunately for most of the congregation, Arabic numerals were used for the pages which were indexed. Only 23 of its hymns appeared in the 1916 edition of *Hymns Ancient and Modern*, including six by Charles Wesley; the remaining 72 were often characterised by doggerel verse and grim conceptions of man's relationship to God. So, not surprisingly, there were six funeral hymns as against five for Christmas, of which only Wesley's 'Hark the Herald Angels Sing' would now be regarded as

Seraphine 1840 (Metropolitan Museum of Art, New York). The Churchwardens of Kirby le Soken purchased an instrument of this kind in 1839 to be played by a professional musician.

a carol. The free translations of the psalms were put into rhyming verse, usually in ballad form.

The Reverend William Coxhead, curate of Kirby le Soken from 1842, was a priest of sincere faith and trust in God's goodness, possessing its practical application in the act of worship, characteristic of the graduates of Trinity College, Cambridge who sought ordination. According to the bishop's instructions, Holy Communion was celebrated eight times a year, including Feast days, so leaving Morning Service at 10.30 and Evening Service at 3 p.m. as the main acts of Sunday worship. Whatever the calibre of the choir in the west gallery, for the next twenty years in or adjoining the chancel, were plenty of young voices provided by the large families of John Dennis Daniels, Richard Stone of Willow Farm, Richard Stone of Frinton Hall and of the curate himself. Numbers were depleted when the boys went away to school. Thanks to the Reverend William Burgess, over half the pews were open benches and the closed pews three feet nine inches high (just over a metre) provided a limited obstacle to congregational worship and were swept away in the alterations completed by 16th January, 1874 when in the body of the church, open pews were installed and the west gallery taken down. The pews in the chancel, across which (according to his daughter) Henry, son of Richard Stone of Frinton Hall, had 'made eyes' at his future wife Mary Holroyd Coxhead, were replaced by choir stalls and the parish church of Kirby le Soken rededicated to Saint Michael. It seems appropriate that the architect who designed the 1872-74 rebuilding, which finally expressed congregational involvement, was that same Henry Stone.

APPENDIX

Sacred Music at the Opening of Kirby Church,
Wednesday, 16th October, at 3 p.m.

Between the Lessons
An Anthem, taken from Psalm C (Cole)
Chorus, 'O be joyful in the Lord' etc.
Duet, 'Be Ye Sure etc' Trio, 'Be thankful unto him' etc. Duet,
'For the Lord is gracious' etc.
Chorus 'Glory be to the Father'.

Before the Litany
An Anthem, taken from Psalm LV (Kent).
Duet, 'Hear my prayer' etc. Solo, 'Take Heed unto me' etc.
Recitative, 'My heart is disquieted etc.
Duet, 'And I said' etc. Chorus, 'O that I had wings like a dove'.

Before the Sermon
Solo (Handel), 'Lord, remember David; teach him to know
thy ways. O guide his tongue with meekness to sing thy praise,
Lord' etc.
Chorus (Kent), 'O speak good of the Lord all ye works of his, in all
places of his dominion. Praise thou the Lord, O my soul. O my
soul, praise the Lord'.

After the Sermon
Anthem taken from I Chronicles XXIX (Kent)
Chorus, 'Blessed be thou, Lord God of Israel our Father, for ever
and ever'.
Quartett, 'Thine, O Lord, is the greatness, and the power, and the
glory, and the victory and the majesty: for all that is in the heaven
and earth is thine; thine is the kingdom, O Lord, and thou art
exalted as Head above all'. Duet, 'Both riches and honour come of
Thee, and Thou reignest over all; and in Thine hand is power and
might; and in Thine hand is to make great, and to give strength
unto all'. Chorus, 'Now therefore, our God, we thank Thee, and
praise Thy Glorious Name'.

II *Life in the Village*

> *"The abominable Free Trade being persisted in,*
> *made it very hard and cruel to all engaged in the*
> *culture of the Soil and the greatest distress and*
> *privation was felt among that respectable body of*
> *the community and all others depending on*
> *them."*
>
> *(Richard Stone of Frinton Hall, 1851)*

By the 1840's the discipline and sense of congregational unity was
enhanced by regular visitations by bishops and archdeacons and
non-resident priests were frowned upon. The three Sokens within

the Bishopric of London received the 1842 Charge of Bishop Bloomfield which laid down guide lines for the behaviour of clergy and congregation in religious worship. As early as 1822, clergy at Kirby had worn a white surplice while conducting a service and 'dressed in a peculiar habit so as to be distinguished from the laity': a black suit with a long coat fastened at the neck, with a starched white linen cravat, of which the Bishop approved. But Bishop Bloomfield required a use of ceremonial which would bring our church to the very verge of popery and to which William Burgess objected. Fortunately, however, a confrontation was avoided by force of circumstances; like other parishes in Essex and Hertfordshire, Kirby became the victim of industrial progress. The Church of England, anxious about the densely populated areas on the East of London and still part of Essex, decided that these areas needed more attention from the Bishop of London, and by Order in Council from 1st January, 1846, transferred what amounted to rural Essex and Hertfordshire to the Bishop of Rochester in Kent. From the beginning, there were problems. In Kent, south of the Thames estuary, only the cathedral town of Rochester was within the Bishopric and the journey to the main part of the diocese was long and difficult. To solve the problem a palace was purchased well outside Chelmsford at Danbury Place for the bishop's residence north of the Thames, and it says much for the dedication of the Bishop of Rochester, whom Burgess admired, that in addition to annual Confirmation services, he made triennial visitations in his unwieldy diocese. On such occasions, the churchwardens of the Sokens attended the bishop's court, once their vicar was too frail to travel.

After fourteen years of uncertainty, in 1844 the Act for the Abolition of Peculiar Jurisdictions was passed by the House of Lords but delayed in the Commons. With major national economic and social reforms occupying Peel's Conservative government, the prime minister announced that 'the Bill is dropped for the present session'. But William Burgess warned the churchwardens in 1846 that the suppression of ecclesiastical courts was inevitable. When the change came in 1858, the government avoided abolishing the courts but allowed them 'to expire by curtailing their business'. By act of Parliament a new court of Probate took over 'proving Wills or granting Letters of Administration and all such business arising out of the same' with one central court of Probate and forty district courts; Essex was divided between London and Ipswich. A court for Divorce and Matrimonial Causes was set up, but marriage licences 'continued to be granted as if it had not been passed'. So by 1862 when the Reverend William Burgess died, the business of the Commissary court of the Sokens had withered away, a fact recognised in his will by the separation of the three parishes Thorpe, Kirby and Walton to remain in the gift of the Elizabeth Burgess Trust on his wife's death.

Once his conflict with the vicar over the rebuilding of Kirby church was resolved, Samuel Baker senior continued to play an important role in parish affairs: overseer of the poor and then guardian, surveyor of the highways and sometimes people's churchwarden. By 1835, when Richard Stone of Frinton Hall

Richard Stone of Frinton Hall 1809-1892. The 'Churchwarden's Books' that he kept for 54 years at Frinton has provided much valuable local evidence, mainly of Kirby le Soken.

Henry Stone 1838-1921 son of Richard and Mary of Frinton Hall. Architect of the Rebuilding of Saint Michael's, Kirby le Soken 1873 and Frinton Church.

Dr. Robert Large Baker (1819- *Mary Holroyd Coxhead aged 18*
85) at Bordsley. Son of Samuel *when Governess in Brighton.*
and Mary of Birch Hall and *1867 married Henry Stone,*
Meers Farm. 1841 House *Architect.*
Surgeon at the Essex and
Colchester Hospital.

married Mary Rand and John Phipps became parish clerk, Samuel Baker Junior had emigrated to Canada. Already in 1830, when still a few months under age, he had been bound over at quarter sessions on his father's surety of twenty pounds to keep the peace 'especially towards George Garrett Husker Munnings of Thorpe, Gentleman', but at the end of the year was an active special constable during the Tendring riots. Unlike his father William, Samuel made no arrangements for the marriage of his three daughters (Mary Ann, Sarah and Fanny) and provided training only for the doctor Robert Large and apprenticeship for John who became a draper in Marylebone; Frederick, the youngest, emigrated to New Zealand. The task of Samuel's unmarried sons, Henry, William and Alfred, was to farm their father's thousand acres (1841), which provided work for forty labourers, three of whom worked for Samuel consistently and maintained an almost privileged relationship with their employer. Samuel Baker of Lower Street was given the largest share of road work whenever his master was surveyor of the highways; the Brackenbury family lived on the Frinton Road with John working at Birch Hall where by 1851 his wife and one of his daughters were indoor servants. Most important of all, the Carringtons rented a cottage from Samuel on Lower Street, Abraham stood by him at the confrontation with the Tendring rioters and Margaret, after nursing her master during his final illness, was present at his death. After Fanny's death at the age of twenty five, in 1846 the thirty year old Sarah eloped to London to marry Lawrence Salmon, son of Samuel's friend Joseph, the successful builder of Beaumont; there the couple lived in an Aldersgate lodging house before finally emigrating to Melbourne. In the 1840's, Samuel's farming interests centred at Birch Hall expanded into West Tilbury where he established William to manage West Tilbury Hall Farm while Henry managed Meers Farm, composed of lands rented in Frinton and the Sokens of Kirby and Walton.

Samuel's relationship with his sisters Mary and Elizabeth was a close one. Mary and her husband, Thomas Stone of Heron House, Horndon on the Hill, kept Samuel in touch with his missionary half-brother in South India which repudiates the claim of the Reverend Henry Baker Senior that his family had cast him off. Elizabeth's younger son, Philip Baker Smith of Great Clacton was an executor for both Samuel and his widow. Both uncle and nephew were staunch supporters of the newly formed Conservative Party created by Sir Robert Peel and were stewards at the Chelmsford public dinner on 22nd September, 1841 to celebrate the party's overwhelming victory in the general election.

By 1831, the fifty one year old Richard Stone had made three marriages and was raising a young family, by his third wife Rebecca (daughter of Edmund Blowers, the collar maker) twenty years his junior. In contrast to the policy of Samuel Baker who controlled his farming kingdom, Richard Stone transferred one thousand pounds for his eldest son Richard to take over the lease of

Nunquam Non Paratus

The Arms of the Stone Family
Drawn by Myra Wilkins.

the farmland centred on Frinton Hall, together with the house, so making possible the profitable marriage with Mary Rand. William, the brother of Richard Stone the elder, also lived at Kirby le Soken and provides an interesting example of the effects of living purely on capital: he held no office in the parish; the three daughters severally married the village grocer, a plumber and a carpenter; one able-bodied son ended in Tendring union workhouse. In his old age he shared a cottage with the widower carpenter and both William and his children were glad to receive a joint of pork at Christmas from Richard Stone of Frinton Hall. Although Frinton was a separate parish with its own dilapidated little church which still stands at the bottom of what is now Connaught Avenue, its 43 parishioners saw little of their rector and lord of the manor, which explains why the Stones of Frinton Hall worshipped at Kirby le Soken; only for baptisms, marriages and sometimes burials was a local priest especially engaged. In 1836, when the Frinton parish clerk demanded the Frinton churchyard for cultivation, the angry Richard Stone took over the job himself and in 1843 became its churchwarden, entering the churchyard from the grounds of Frinton Hall which is now demolished. As a result of his efforts, 'the little sanctuary' as Richard Stone called the Frinton parish church, was rebuilt in 1868. The policy of all the Richard Stones both at Willow Farm and Frinton Hall was to include among their indoor servants, at least two labourers, one a shepherd. The Torrance family enjoyed a long period of service with the Stones: Richard came from Cavendish, Suffolk via Great Holland, from Michaelmas 1801, 'letting himself to Richard Stone of Frinton Hall and lodging at his master's farm in the Parish of Kirby'. By 1851, the Torrance family rented a cottage on Frinton Road, Kirby with the men working at Willow Farm and two daughters (dairymaid and housemaid) at Frinton Hall.

Although the abolition of his power as Commissary was of great moment to the vicar, Kirby villagers were concerned with more practical problems. Within four months of each other, the Lord of the Sokens, Benjamin Chapman, issued coroner's certificates for the burial of a labourer's two children: eleven year old John was killed by a waggon during the 1832 harvesting and at the end of the year his younger brother, Timothy, was burned to death. During the 1840's and 1850's, the congregation (mostly of labourers'

Meers Farm built by Samuel Baker in 1851. Demolished 1979 to make way for a Housing Estate.

families) increased at the Primitive Methodist Church in Upper Kirby, which could baptise their children but was unable to bury their dead. At the turn of the year 1840 to '41, within a few days of each other, the child daughters of Robert and Susan Mumford died of scarlet fever at Kirby Hall. On the lighter side, in the autumn following, a seal was sighted off the coast of Walton. With friends, Robert Mumford went out in a small yacht and maintained his reputation as a marksman by shooting the seal through the head. To their great satisfaction, the seal provided upwards of 70 pounds of meat, 10 quarts of oil and the skin was dressed by Mr. Page of Maningtree to make a wrap to keep Mr. Mumford warm. On 25th April, 1843, the London parish of Saint Boltolph-without-Bishopsgate ordered the removal from its workhouse of John Phipp's daughter Eliza 'aged about 26 years an unmarried woman now about eight months gone with child' to the parish of Kirby; the infant was born in the Tendring union workhouse. On the night of 10th November, 1844, a brig on fire on the Gunfleet Sands lit up the area to the alarm of Kirby inhabitants who feared that Frinton Hall was burning down. The suicide of Thomas Hammond, aged

36, one time tenant of the 'Hare and Hounds' in Upper Kirby and a higgler who attended Colchester market regularly, makes grim reading. After an unusually violent quarrel with his wife, he hanged himself in the privy. At the inquest the verdict of 'felo de se' was returned, 'The deceased having destroyed himself whilst of sound mind, memory and understanding'. Late on Saturday night, 12th April Thomas Hammond was buried on the edge of Kirby churchyard with no religious rites.

As in most parts of the country, a succession of bad harvests to 1845 brought distress to the agricultural population until the mild winter of 1846:

> 'January was remarkably mild. The wheats grew all winter and roses bloomed outdoors. Turnips and most green crops were plentiful (very providentially for the poor) as owing to the wet of last Summer, the potato crop was a general failure all over the United Kingdom — as well as the continent of Europe, but the August and September drought and the severe winter that followed pushed up wheat prices.'

In his churchwarden book, Richard Stone continues, describing the effects of free trade:

> 'The year 1850 proved a trying one for farmers and many were ruined by the wicked and unjust system of Free Trade and the poor labourers found to their cost that bread might be dear at one penny a loaf, if they lacked the penny to procure it.'

In 1852, able bodied men earned 8 shillings and 6 pence (42½ new pence) a week as compared with prices:

Bread—5 pence per quartern loaf (2 large loaves)
Beef, veal and pork—5 pence per pound
Mutton—7 pence per pound
Lamb—8 pence per pound
Wool—1 shilling per pound

At this time of social and economic change, on 15th June, 1852 Samuel Baker died of inflammation of the bladder, aged 66. Two days before his death, with his wife and solicitor as witnesses, he gave instructions for the disposal of his £14,000 estate; no will was made, which meant the necessity of a sworn statement by the witnesses before the Reverend William Burgess, acting as commissioner for oaths. The settlement left Mrs. Mary Baker in virtual control of the estate, with William at West Tilbury and Henry at Meers Farm accountable to the executors. Each child was left £600 with repayments to the estate from those who had already received more than their share during their father's lifetime. The runaway Sarah (or her children after her death) was to be paid the interest on her share 'for her own particular use'. Not surprisingly, the settlement resulted in family conflict, so much so that Mrs. Baker's will, proved in 1864, instructs the executors to disinherit any child disputing its terms. The building of the 'beautiful' mansion of Meers Farm with its outbuildings completed in 1851 (demolished in 1979 to make way for a bungalow estate) was expensive, so reducing the final share-out on the death of Samuel's wife. With their father gone, both William and Henry married within a year: Henry, discreetly by Special Licence to Jane, daughter of George Low of Blue House, Walton at St. Dunstan in the West, Fleet Street. Not until October, 1854 did Alfred, aged 29, marry Maria Dennis Daniels, aged 23 — a union between two Kirby families that, on the surface, seemed full of promise.

Life in Kirby changed after 1852 with the new problems faced by men and women that lacked the confidence of their predecessors. Already, Jeremiah Foaker had been replaced by John Salmon (of Great Oakley) at Sneating Hall and by John Dennis Daniels of Brick Barn as vicar's warden. The year 1852 brought not only the death of Samuel Baker, but that of John Daniels for so long the centre of Kirby traffic (post, carrier, coach, poor relief and parish register entries), followed two months later by the stalwart widow, Mrs. Elizabeth Riddelsdell whose blacksmith's business was taken over by her journeyman, William Oxborrow. Only Robert Mumford and John Dennis Daniels remained of the older generation for, after two years, died the widow of Richard Stone of Willow Farm, leaving her stepson at Frinton Hall, as joint executor, to supervise her farm and educate her children.

This generation of younger men administering Kirby knew little of the local benevolent despotism of their parents; increasingly the government at Westminster controlled their lives and taxed their incomes already depleted by ancient tithes, increasing poor rate and the effects of the new policy of free trade.

CHAPTER EIGHT

I *The Bakers of India*

*'My work is still with the natives. I feel the same
loyalty to Church Missionary principles I felt
when I gave up the Living in 1862 my dying friend
pressed upon me.'*
(Rev. Henry Baker Junior to the C.M.S.
Secretary, December, 1876.)

From the beginning, Kirby le Soken had responded to 'the
Evangelical outcry for . . . Indian Missions'. In Travancore
(present day Kerala), the work of Samuel Baker's half-brother, the
Reverend Henry Baker, and his descendants flourished until the
end of the century. After the death of his infant son in the 1860
cholera epidemic in Mundeyum, the Rev. Henry Baker Junior
returned to England for two years not only to visit the Rev. William
Burgess as well as his daughters at the C.M.S. School, but also to
raise funds for training ten young hill Arians from Travancore as
teachers of the inhabitants of the western slopes of the Ghats
Mountains. After preaching at the Sokens in 1861, he became
curate of Plaistow, the dockland area of the parish of West Ham,
where he published a small book, *'The Hill Arians of Travancore
and the Progress of Christianity Among Them'* (Macintosh and
Hunt — London 1862), describing his work. William Burgess was
anxious for him to take over the Thorpe living after his death, but
Henry refused. By the autumn, when the missionary and two
daughters returned to Travancore, the Reverend William Burgess
was dead.

One of the most successful ventures of the Baker family in the
Pallam area was the girls' boarding school in Kottayam begun in

The Reverend Henry Baker, half brother of Samuel of Birch Hall. (Reputedly painted by a Dutch Sea Captain.) From December 1817 he lived and worked in Pallam until his death in 1888, establishing a large Christian Centre in Travancore.

1827 by Mrs. Baker Senior by boarding girls as part of her household. By 1873, the school had over 139 pupils and was run by Mary Frances, the eldest daughter of Henry Baker Junior, after working with her mother for some years. However, because she was a woman, she remained unrecognised as a missionary by the C.M.S. until 1893 (a year before the School's Jubilee). Upon her death in 1901, the School was the chief beneficiary and she expressed the hope that 'it will be called The Baker Memorial School'; the plaque put up in the entrance hall commemorated the Baker origin in Kirby le Soken, Essex. In 1867, after his father's death, the Rev. Henry Baker reported that the congregation at Pallam had multiplied over twenty five times since he had taken charge in 1844 and that they 'were gradually working out caste feeling' which existed even among the Arian Christians. After a short visit to England in 1877 (when he probably attended his brother's wedding in North Shoebury) he died in the following year in Madras after a lifetime devoted to the religious, medical and educational welfare of the people of the coast and western hills of Travancore.

The missionary families of the Kirby-born Reverend Henry Baker and his children returned to England to be educated and sometimes to find a wife. With the declining health of William Burgess, they looked to the social circle of the farmer, Thomas Stone of Heron House, East Horndon and his wife Mary. In 1845, this group was enlarged by the marriage of their daughter Ann to George Alexander Clark of Moat Hall, North Shoebury, and then by their married son Henry farming at Wick Farm, Wickford. In 1855, the Church Missionary Society agreed that the Senior Rev. Henry Baker's widowed daughter, Amelia, should return to England not only for her health, but 'to make friends for' her eldest son, John Henry Johnson who was old enough to leave the C.M.S. Home in Highbury and begin a career in England. The fourteen year old boy was befriended by the nephew of the recently widowed Mary Stone, Doctor Robert Large Baker, F.R.C.S. (1861); L.S.A., practising in Bordesley on the outskirts of Birmingham, and, thanks to him, spent eight months with Messrs. Udd and Symonds, factors of Birmingham before becoming apprenticed to the National Provincial Bank of Birmingham until November, 1861 when he became a clerk in the cashier's department of the Bank of England. There, he was promoted principal of the cashier's store office in 1901, finally retiring in March, 1906. In 1869 Mr. Johnson married Alice Mary, daughter of Henry Stone of Wickford and created a union between the two main branches of the Baker family, which was further cemented by the marriage in 1877 of his uncle Alfred George Baker, widower and planter of Komorate to Fanny Clark of North Shoebury. The grandson of this marriage, Mr. Robert Baker, returned in 1962 with his family to farm in Essex, but still retaining the limited interests in Kerala allowed by the Indian authorities.

II *Enterprise in England*

*'I shall strive to do the best in my power to raise
my position in life, the same as you have done.'
(James Robert — letter to parents Dr Robert
Large and Mrs Baker — Melbourne 23.3.1866)*

The leading families of Kirby le Soken formed part of the general exodus of its inhabitants. With the expiry of the tenancy of Birch Hall in 1861, Samuel Baker's widow moved to 36 Head Street, Colchester with her daughter. Once the eldest son, William, had completed farming in West Tilbury, Essex, under the terms of his father's will, he moved with his family to the larger Pitsea Manor Farm which he farmed for the rest of his life until 1885. But by 1861, Alfred, calling himself a 'farmer' was living with his wife Maria Dennis and two children in a small terraced house near the end of Saville Street, Walton. By 1863, his mother had paid off his debts and met his funeral expenses, to be deducted from his widow's inheritance; to make a living, Maria kept a lodging house in Walton until 1886 when a legacy from her father made it possible to open apartments in the newly developed Clacton-on-Sea at 5 Marine Parade where she died in 1895, apparently ostracised by both Bakers and Daniels. After his mother's death in 1874, John took the Baker family Bible to South Africa where he emigrated with his second wife and family and died at Humansdorp, Cape Province in 1878 in the same month as his niece Mary Jane was married in Kirby le Soken. Mary Jane's father, Henry, alone remained to farm there at Meer's Farm until his premature death in 1876. However, the new railway system made it possible for his widow Jane to maintain close links with her brother-in-law Doctor Robert Large Baker of Leamington, who acted in loco parentis when Mary Jane married Axel Frederick Ericson, Merchant Clerk of Newcastle on Tyne; their only daughter died unmarried. Surprisingly, the terms of Jane Baker's will encouraged her two sons to farm: Frederick at The Hall in Great Holland from which he emigrated to New Zealand with his wife and most of his adult family after the 1914-18 War; Maurice at Meers Farm, and with his death in 1935, the Baker family in Kirby le Soken became extinct.

The former house surgeon of Colchester hospital, Robert Large Baker, after marrying his first cousin Emma, practised at 113 High Street, Bordesley, Birmingham for over twenty years, becoming a F.R.C.S. in 1861 and a Doctor of Medicine of Saint Andrew's University in 1866. By 1870, when he retired to Leamington, Dr. Baker was supporting Mr Middlemore's Emigration Homes (a successful Birmingham venture to take destitute children off the streets, and bring them up to find a new life in Australia or Canada) and was a director of the newly formed Birmingham Wagon Co. Ltd., and of The Patent Railway Axle Box Company, Birmingham. In addition, by 1885 he had assembled a botanical collection which was 'one of the most splendid and complete in the country'. In 1874 he published *'A Catalogue of Plants Collected in Warwickshire'* compiled with the help of the Rugby School Natural History Society, so inevitably he became a member of the Jephson Garden Committee to design the park now in the centre of Leamington. A wealthy doctor, businessman and philanthropist, in 1871 Doctor Baker became a member of the house committee from its inception in 1877, in 1878 insituted a nursing home to hire out nurses for private houses with payment and rules controlled by Warneford hospital and was a prime mover in creating the local charity organisation. To his funeral in 1885, the dignitaries of Warwickshire came to pay him tribute joined by his great friend, executor and cousin John Henry Johnson and one son, the Reverend Samuel Howard Baker. At the end of the first world war, Doctor Robert Large Baker's grandaughter, May Victoria Howard Baker, private secretary to Lord Robert Cecil, attended the Paris peace talks for the Treaty of Versailles (1919) as well as the first two meetings of the League of Nations at Geneva. Once again, the Bakers became linked with India when in 1925 May Victoria married the Indian Civil Servant, James Almond who became judicial commissioner of the North West Frontier Province, was knighted in 1941 and retired to Ross-on-Wye where he became active in local government.

Records of the Dennis Daniels family give the impression of a close knit group. John Dennis Daniels, the founder of the line, remained to farm at Brick Barn until his wife died in 1879, when he moved with his youngest daughter to rooms in the neighbourhood of his son's drapery business in Kentish Town where he died in

1885, a year after the death of his eldest son in New York. In the early 1860's, Alfred and Charles were apprenticed to Drason's, a Linen Draper of Tottenham Court Road, where, like other apprentices, they slept on wooden benches under the counter. In 1866, Charles married into the Nicholson family of Sladbury Farm, Great Clacton, by wedding Charlotte, daughter of George Henry Nicholson who had built up a successful leather business in Bethnal Green Road. In that same year Charles and Alfred opened the first of the shops of C. & A. Daniels at 207 Kentish Town Road to found what was to become the leading family drapers of North West London until after the 1939-45 War. But tuberculosis of the lungs was a powerful enemy: Charles died in 1874 and was replaced by Edward, formerly apprenticed to a tailor and married to Charlotte's sister Alice; when Alice died in 1885, the widower Edward married his widowed sister-in-law. The family fortunes expanded rapidly and the children of these marriages continued the business either in the drapery, or in the leather trade which was

Jane Shum with her mother, Jane, wife of James Shum of Hill House. The family lived at Hill House from about 1850 until Jane died on the 5th of December 1917, aged 72, after showing great generosity to the Parish. The Shum Trust for distribution of money for elderly parishoners at Christmas resulted from her £500 legacy.

given an important boost in the 1914-18 war, bringing a K.B.E. to Percy, the son of Edward and Alice. In 1981, although the drapery stores have been closed for some years, Daniels & Daniels Ltd., now of Leicester, continue the trade in leather.

By 1862, only three children of Richard Stone had survived at Willow Farm when Rebecca Harman Stone left to marry the miller, Henry Beckwith, of Holbrook, Suffolk and Hector remained to farm. But two sons of their elder half brother, Richard Stone of Frinton Hall emigrated to the United States of America: Richard, the eldest, wrote once in 1865, three years after Charles had died at Hagerstown. Henry and Frederick registered in 1864 as Associates of the Royal Institute of British Architects, living and working in London. In 1872 Frederick received the certificate of competency to act as district surveyor in London granted by the R.I.B.A. and because he died intestate and unmarried, the long lost brother Richard was traced and returned from Kansas City for a short visit, over ten years after his father's death in Great Holland in 1892. Henry became the architect of the rebuilt Frinton church, the alterations to St. Michael's, Kirby le Soken and later, of Kirby's first National School and his marriage in 1867 to Mary Holroyd, daughter of the Reverend William Coxhead, was to bring him into close contact with his father-in-law's problems.

The death of the Reverend William Burgess on 29th April, 1862 aged eighty-two provided a landmark for all three Sokens. His will recognised that the claims of the Sokens as a peculiar jurisdiction were no longer valid by making Thorpe, Kirby and Walton into separate, independent parishes to remain in the gift of the widow Mrs. Elizabeth Burgess and subsequently of trustees, named in her will. William Burgess's fortune of £25,000, except for small personal legacies, was held in trust by the widow until her death when the fortune was to be divided between specified religious and social organisations of the Evangelical Church of England, and to a lesser degree, of Essex.

On 13th August, the Reverend William Langston Coxhead, now a widower, was inducted as vicar of the parish of Kirby le Soken which in 1863 received the first visitation of the archdeacon of Colchester for at least forty years. The report was favourable, but within two years, the vicar's mental condition began to deteriorate and ended in his death nine years later from 'Softening of the

Brain' at the age of fifty nine. By the 1865 visitation, the font had disappeared; on 12th December, 1872, William Coxhead signed the parish register for the last time four years after the archdeacon had reported 'the poor worthy vicar is in sad health, his Curate very eccentric, Church deserted'. At first, the parish had managed with local help because the vicar's illness was intermittent, but in 1866 he was forced to employ a curate and moved to Colchester with a crippled daughter and two young children. The other boys dispersed into banking and each of his five daughters earned her living as a governess: Mary Holroyd in Brighton, Amelia Selina at Tranby House, Hessle, Yorkshire and the crippled Augusta combined the task of visiting governess with that of caring for her father. The vicar's health deteriorated rapidly at the end of the decade and on the initiative of Richard Stone of Frinton, the able curate, the Reverend W. G. Stagg, appointed in 1869, began the necessary rebuilding programme, generously supported by the owner of Horsey Island and nearing completion when the vicar died. By 1873, the chancel and nave were restored, the west gallery removed, the church re-pewed and Saint Michael's, Kirby le Soken was re-dedicated with the Reverend W. G. Stagg as vicar.

III   *Decline of Kirby le Soken*

> *'The New Frinton Railway Station is within easy reach by rail and road of the neighbouring places of Clacton-on-Sea and Walton-on-Naze, and of the pretty inland villages of Kirby Cross, Great Holland, Thorpe, Weeley, Great Oakley, Tendring, etc., all of which are equally attractive to the pedestrian, tourist, antiquarian and lovers of the picturesque.'*
> *(Auctioneer's Notice for Sale of Plots of Land: Frinton, 10th September, 1888.)*

The decline in importance of Kirby le Soken was brought about not so much from parochial inertia as from outside factors over which the inhabitants had no control. A year after the death of William Burgess, the Tendring Hundred railway to link Colchester with

Walton (already an established watering place) was opened; on 27th July, 1866, Kirby Cross station was ready and Walton-on-Naze in the following year. Within four days, on 25th May, 1867, with great excitement, Richard Stone and his two daughters were 'taken up and set down' at Frinton level crossing for their first rail journey to Colchester. The development of the railway linked to London, the increasing wealth of the urban middle and working class, together with the topical interest in seaside holidays as conducive to good health (the important Public Health Act was passed in 1875, after much national debate), resulted in the enterprising planning of a holiday centre named Clacton-on-Sea on Great Clacton farmland. In 1878, the parish of Saint Paul, Clacton-on-Sea was created and by 1882, the inconvenience of leaving the train at Weeley to make the last 5½ miles by horsebus or carriage, was overcome by the creation of a terminal station from Thorpe. By 1886, in Frinton the land tilled by Richard Stone and his ancestors for over a hundred years as tenant farmers, was bought by P. Cooper Esquire of Lichfield to establish a first class marine estate. When Frinton station was opened in 1888, between fifty and sixty shops and houses and the Queen's Hotel were already built (in 1904, Station Road was re-named Connaught Avenue). Unlike Kirby, both Clacton-on-Sea and Frinton-on-Sea were supplied with piped water by the Tendring Water Company and provided with gas from Walton. The Eastern Railway Company, together with shipowners, showed great enterprise in organising day trips to Clacton-on-Sea and Walton-on-Naze, bringing an expanding seasonal tourism demanding new amenities.

Thus Kirby le Soken, instead of being the leading parish of the area, was overshadowed by its newly built neighbours and regarded as 'a pretty inland village'. The work of the customs officer, who for generations had lived in Lower Street, was transferred to Walton in 1868 because 'all he had to do was to collect some light dues from vessels visiting ports in Hamford Water in all amounting to five pounds a year'. Even within the parish itself, the importance of the station increased the significance of Kirby Cross, and where the railway led, the automobile followed. So, for its inhabitants, Kirby le Soken became once again 'the village by the Church', and the significance of 'le Soken', once so important, faded into obscurity.

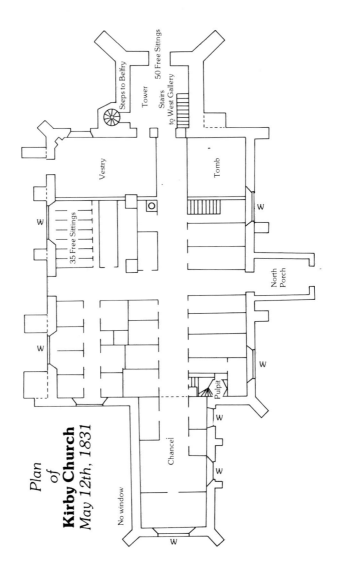

Plan
of
Kirby Church
May 12th, 1831

No window

Chancel

W

W

W

Pulpit

W

North Porch

W

W

Tomb

W

Vestry

35 Free Sittings

W

Steps to Belfry

Tower

Stairs to West Gallery

50 Free Sittings

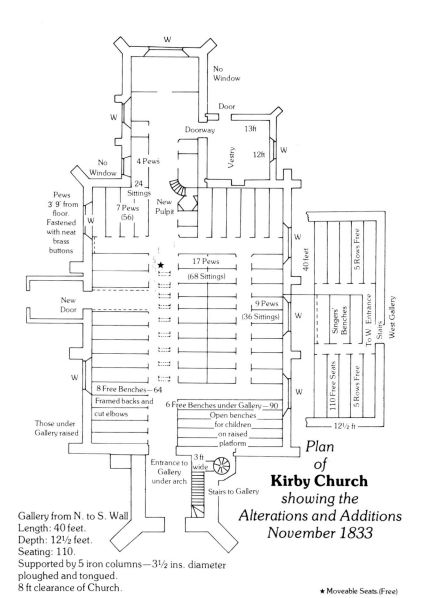

W

No
Window

Door

Doorway

13ft

12ft

W

Vestry

40 feet

5 Rows Free

4 Pews

No
Window

24
Sittings

7 Pews
(56)

New
Pulpit

Pews
3' 9" from
floor.
Fastened
with neat
brass
buttons

★

17 Pews
(68 Sittings)

W

9 Pews
(36 Sittings)

W

Singers'
Benches

To W. Entrance

West Gallery

New
Door

110 Free Seats

5 Rows Free

W

8 Free Benches—64

Framed backs and
cut elbows

6 Free Benches under Gallery—90

Open benches
for children
on raised
platform

12½ ft

Those under
Gallery raised

Entrance to
Gallery
under arch

3 ft
wide

Stairs to Gallery

*Plan
of*
Kirby Church
*showing the
Alterations and Additions
November 1833*

Gallery from N. to S. Wall
Length: 40 feet.
Depth: 12½ feet.
Seating: 110.
Supported by 5 iron columns—3½ ins. diameter
ploughed and tongued.
8 ft clearance of Church.

★ Moveable Seats (Free)

109

TABLE I. THE FAMILY OF SAMUEL BAKER 1783 to 1852 OF MEERS FARM AND BIRCH HALL KIRBY LE SOKEN, ESSEX

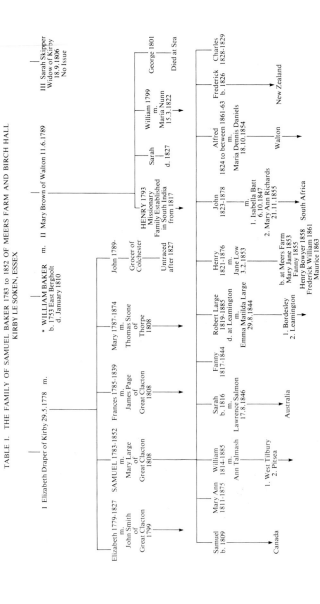

* Children shown who reached adult life.
▲ Known Descendants.

110

Index

Relationship to Samuel Baker (S.B.) shown.

112

114